ALSO BY STANLEY DONWOOD

There Will Be No Quiet

Catacombs of Terror!

Humor

Household Worms

Dead Children Playing

Slowly Downward

BAD ISLAND

•

STANLEY DONWOOD

W. W. NORTON & COMPANY
Independent Publishers Since 1923

First American Edition 2020

Printed in the United States of America

For information about permission to reproduce selections from this book, write to Permissions, W. W. Norton & Company, Inc., 500 Fifth Avenue, New York, NY 10110

For information about special discounts for bulk purchases, please contact W. W. Norton Special Sales at specialsales@wwnorton.com or 800-233-4830

Manufacturing by LSC Communications, Harrisonburg
Production manager: Beth Steidle

Library of Congress Cataloging-in-Publication Data

Names: Donwood, Stanley, author.
Title: Bad island / Stanley Donwood.
Description: First American edition. | New York :
W. W. Norton & Company, 2020.
Identifiers: LCCN 2020009629 | ISBN 9781324001850 (hardcover) |
ISBN 9781324001867 (epub)
Subjects: LCSH: End of the world—Comic books, strips, etc. | Graphic novels.
Classification: LCC PN6737.D66 B33 2020 | DDC 741.5/942—dc23
LC record available at https://lccn.loc.gov/2020009629

W. W. Norton & Company, Inc., 500 Fifth Avenue, New York, N.Y. 10110
www.wwnorton.com

W. W. Norton & Company Ltd., 15 Carlisle Street, London W1D 3BS

1 2 3 4 5 6 7 8 9 0

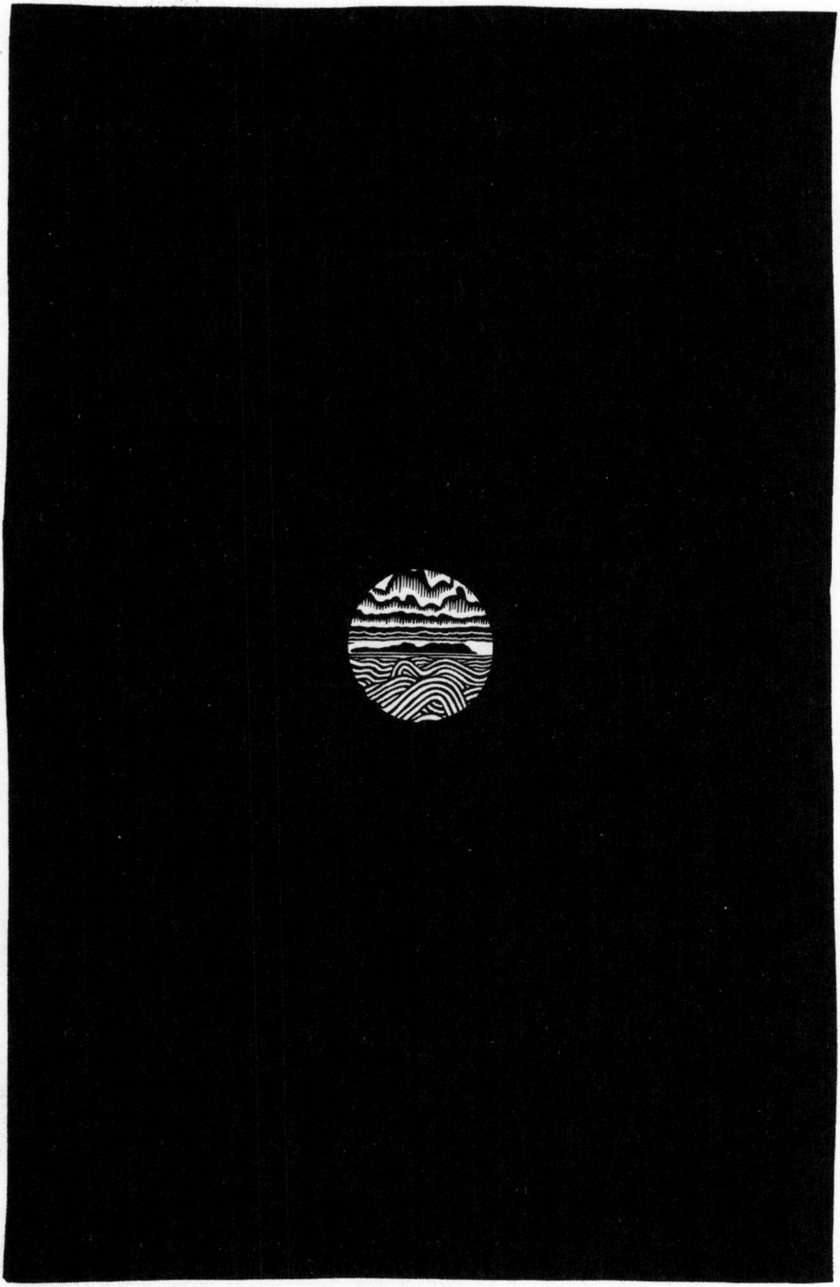

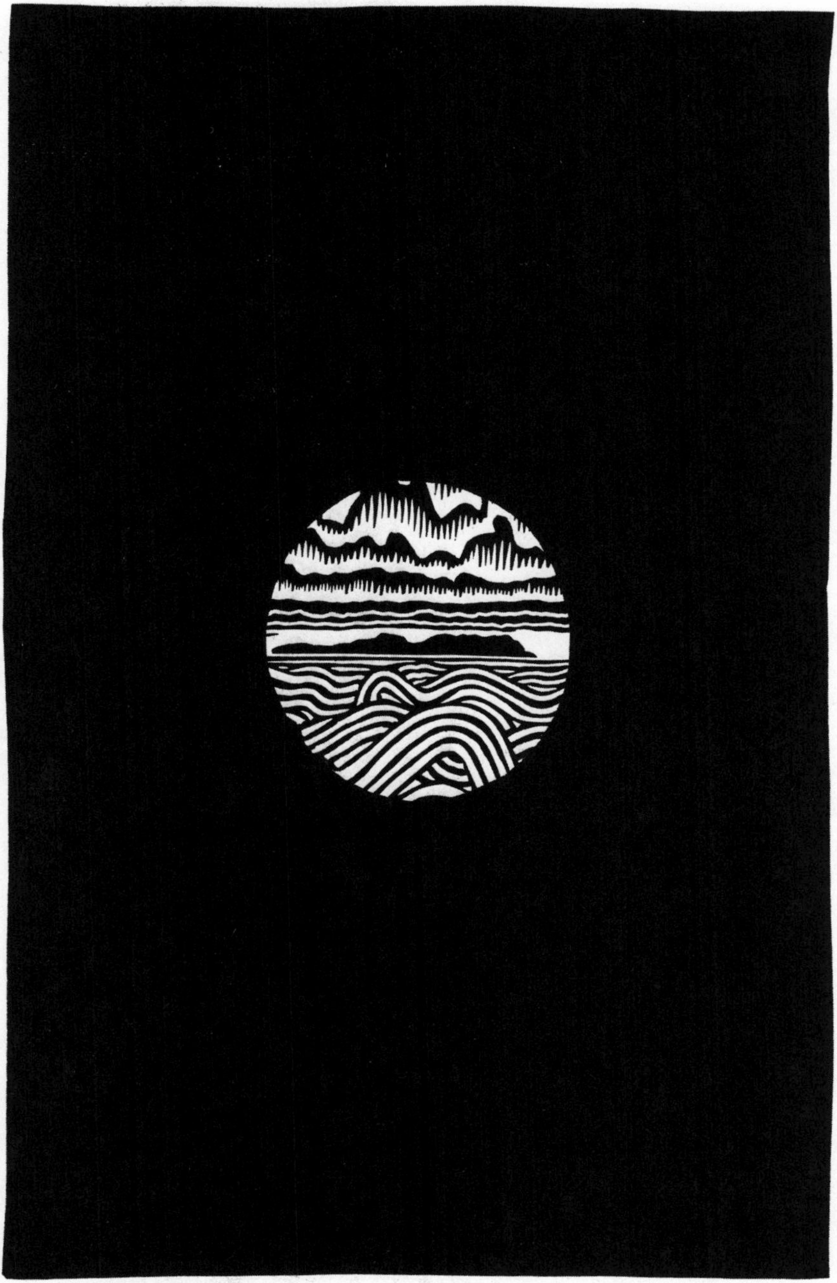

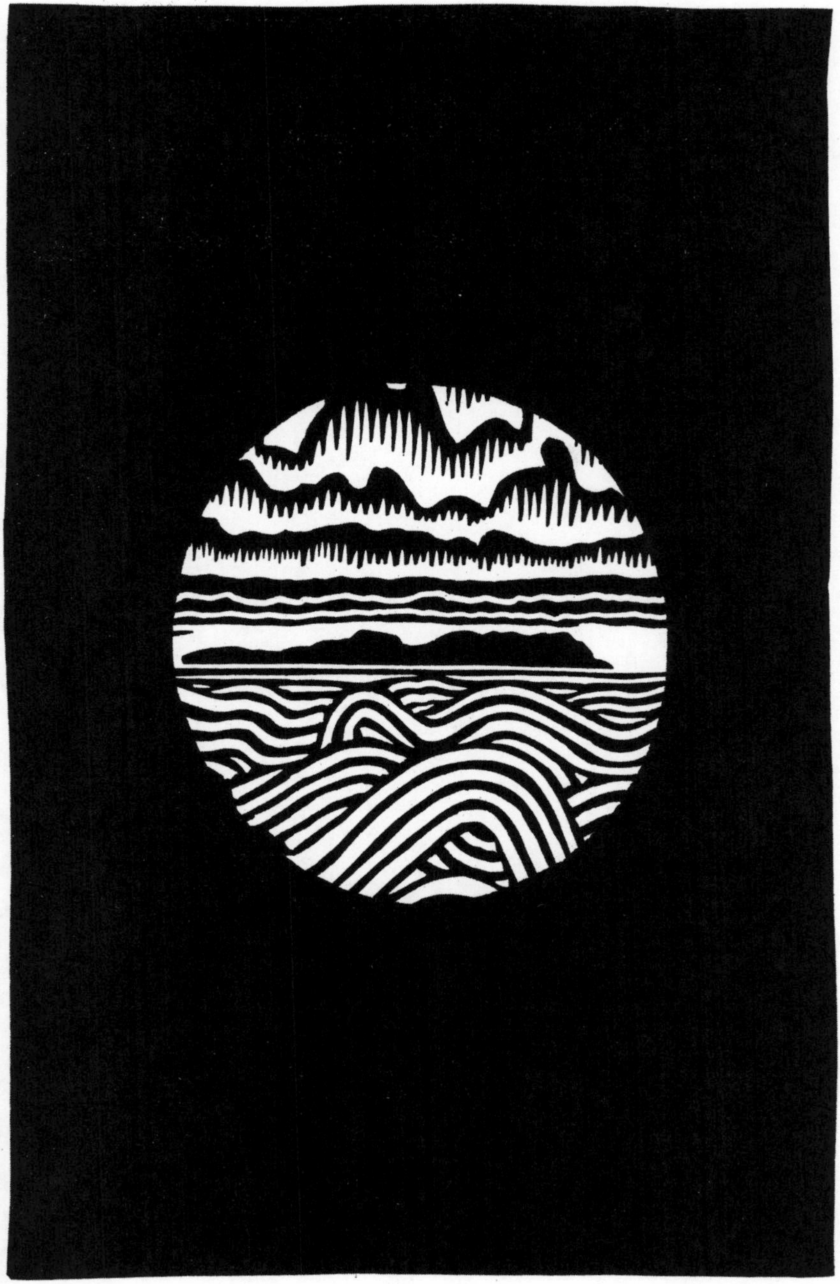

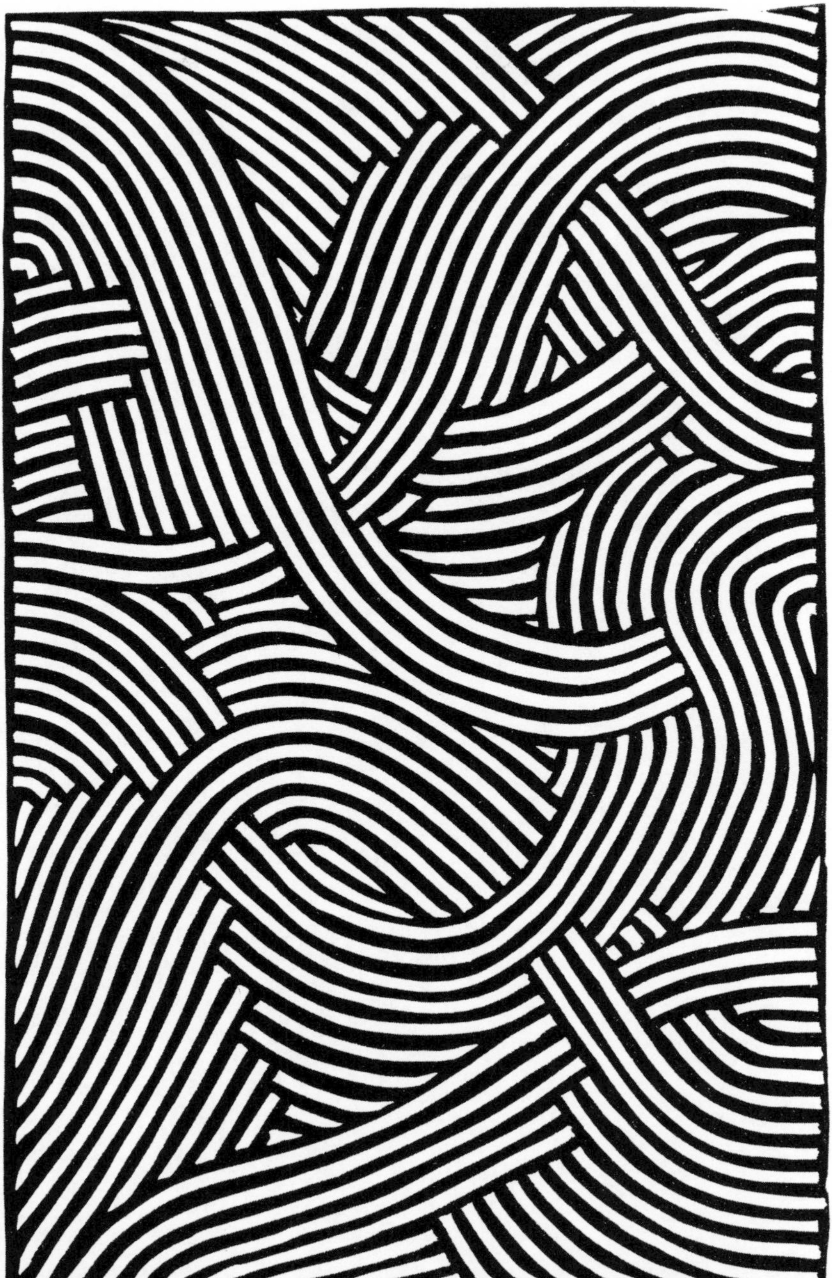

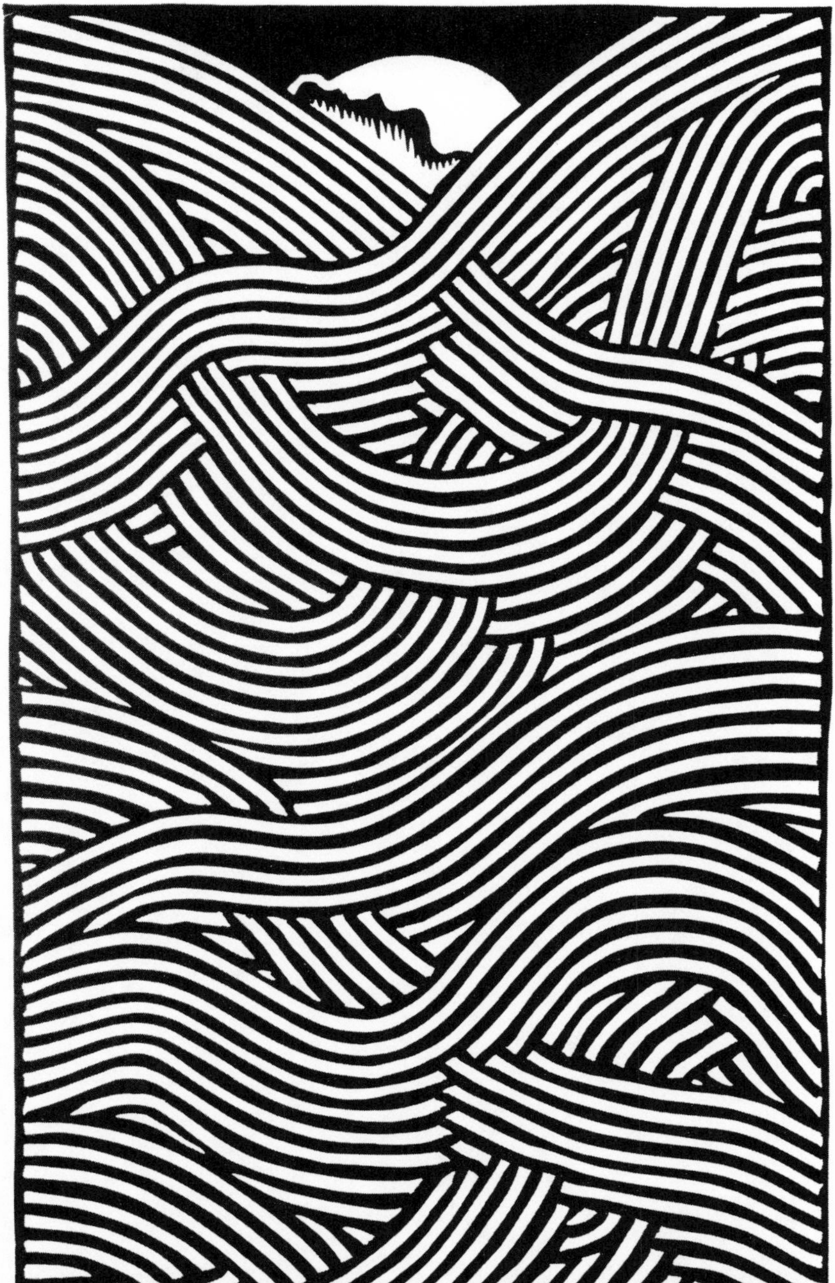

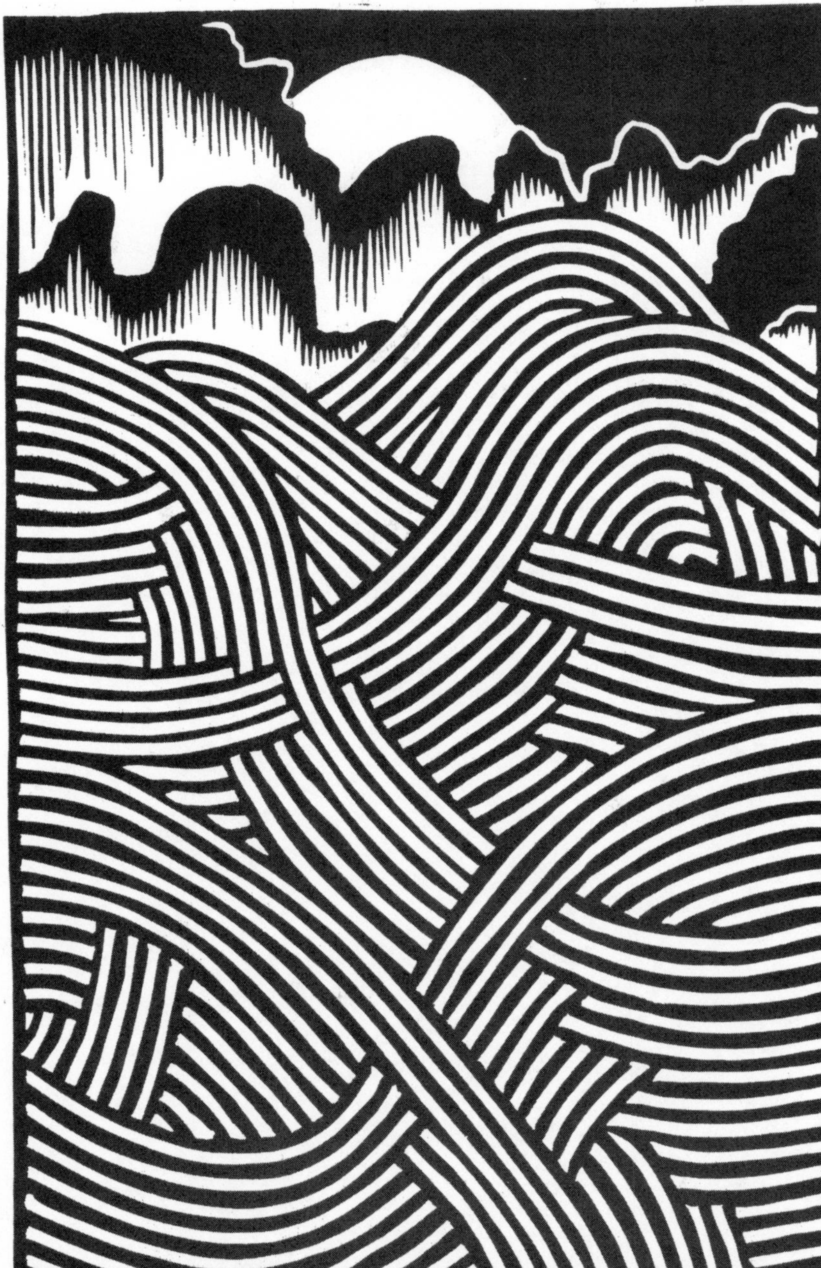

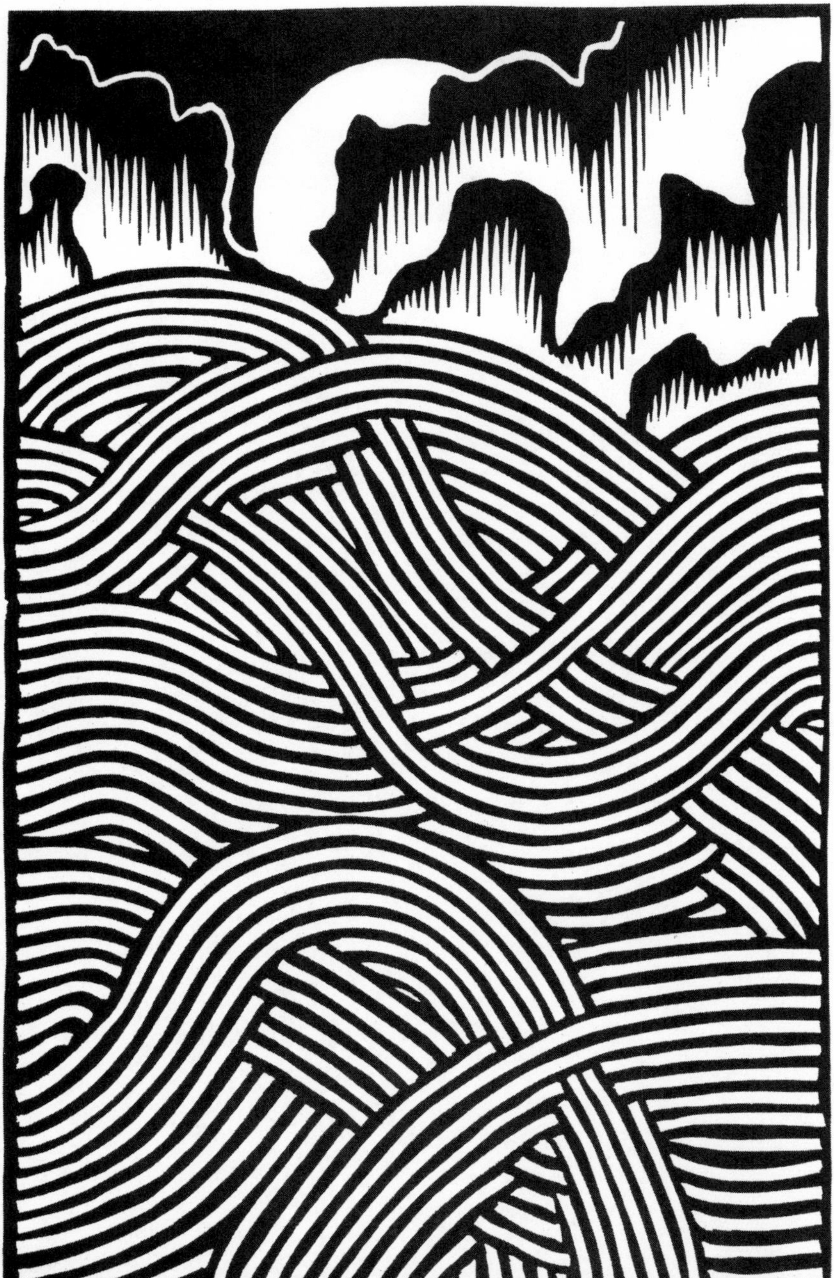

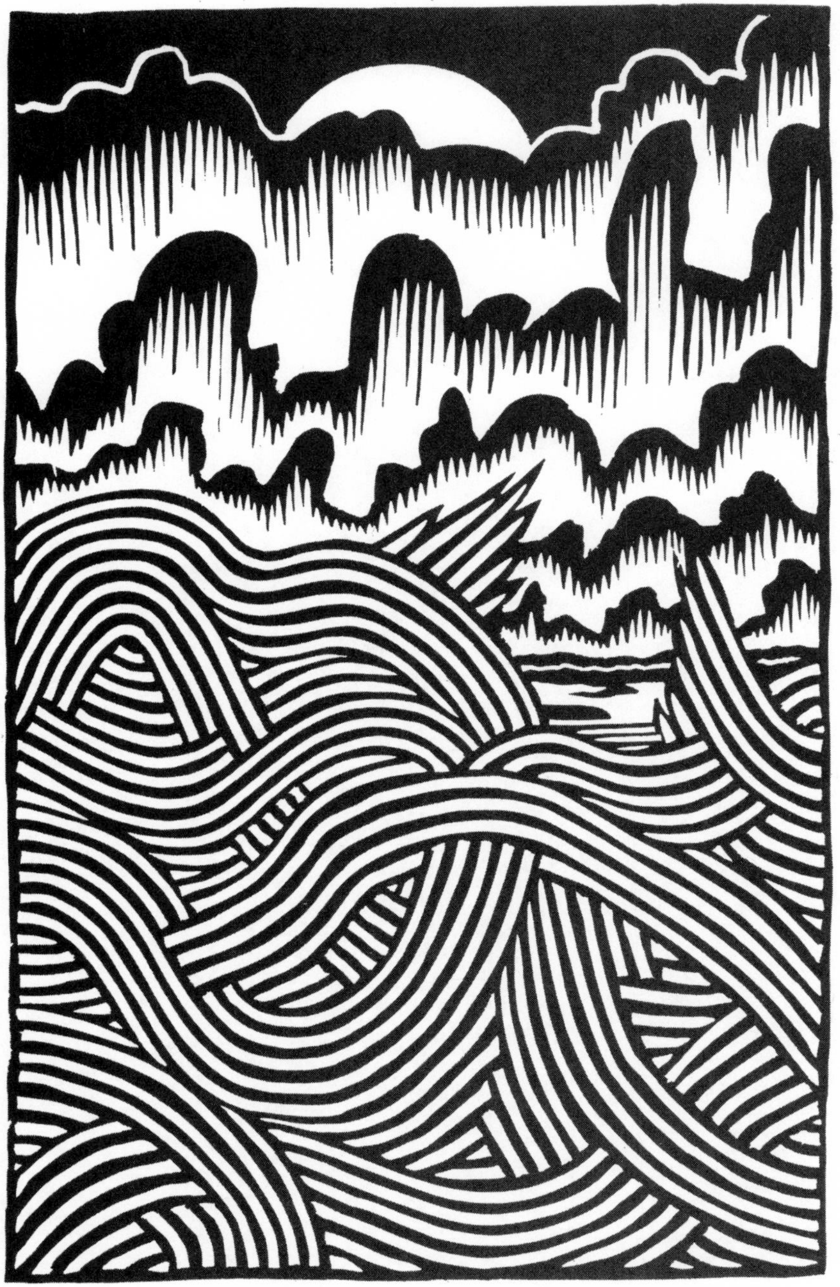

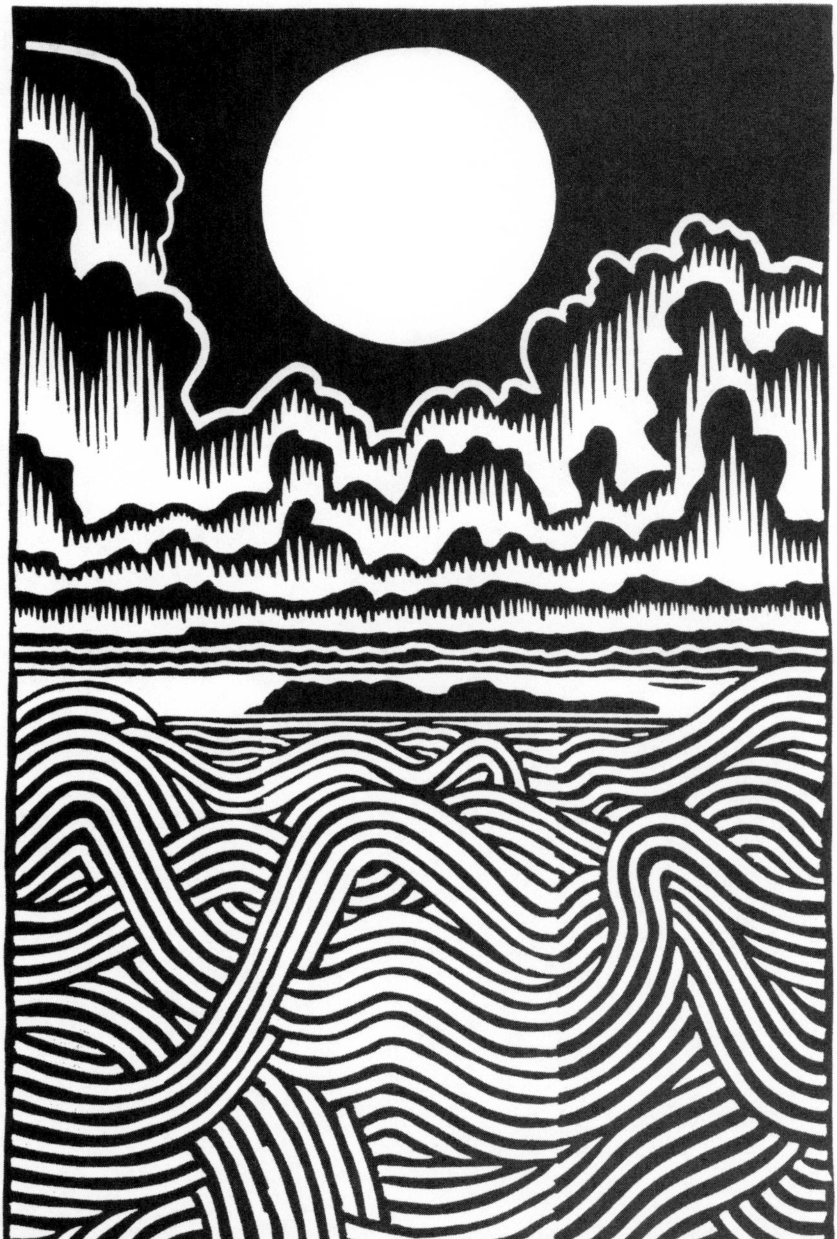

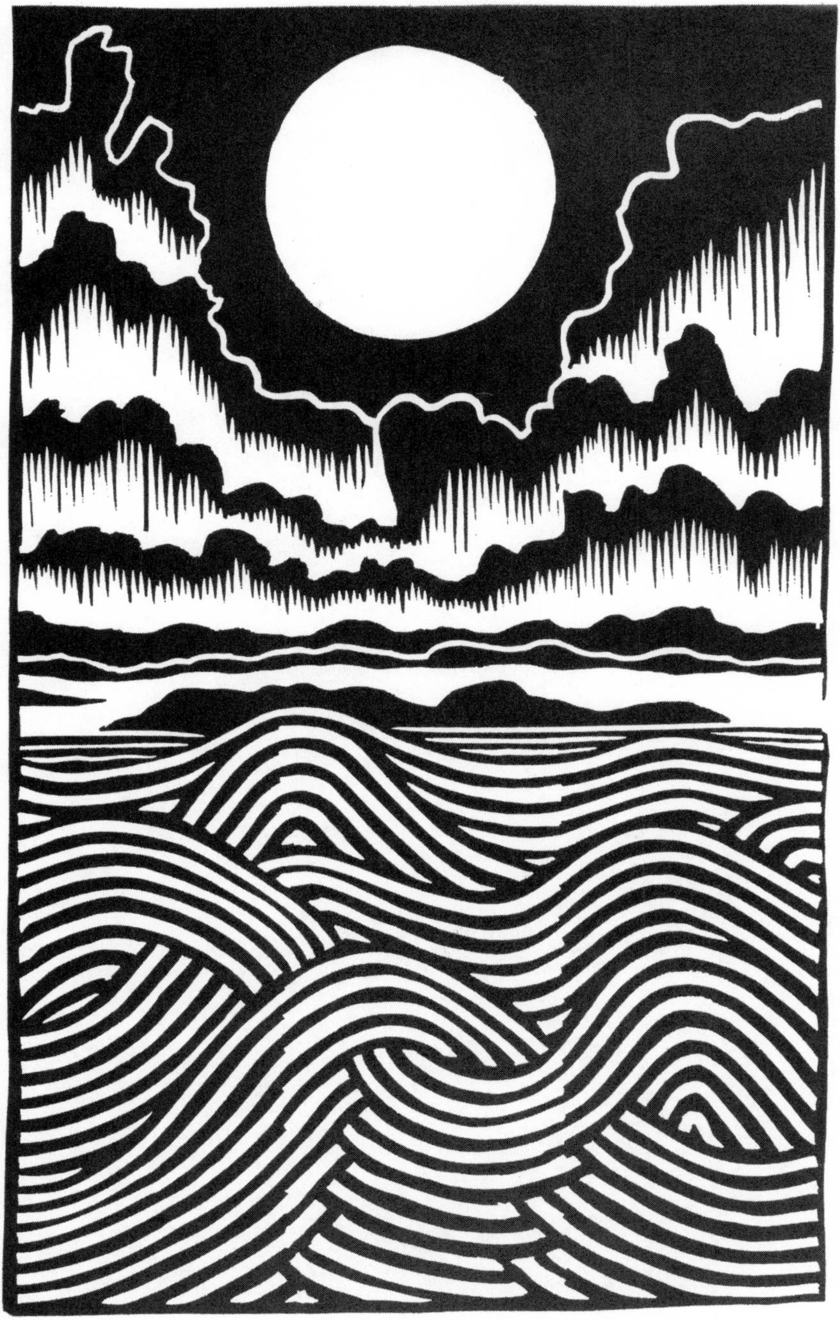

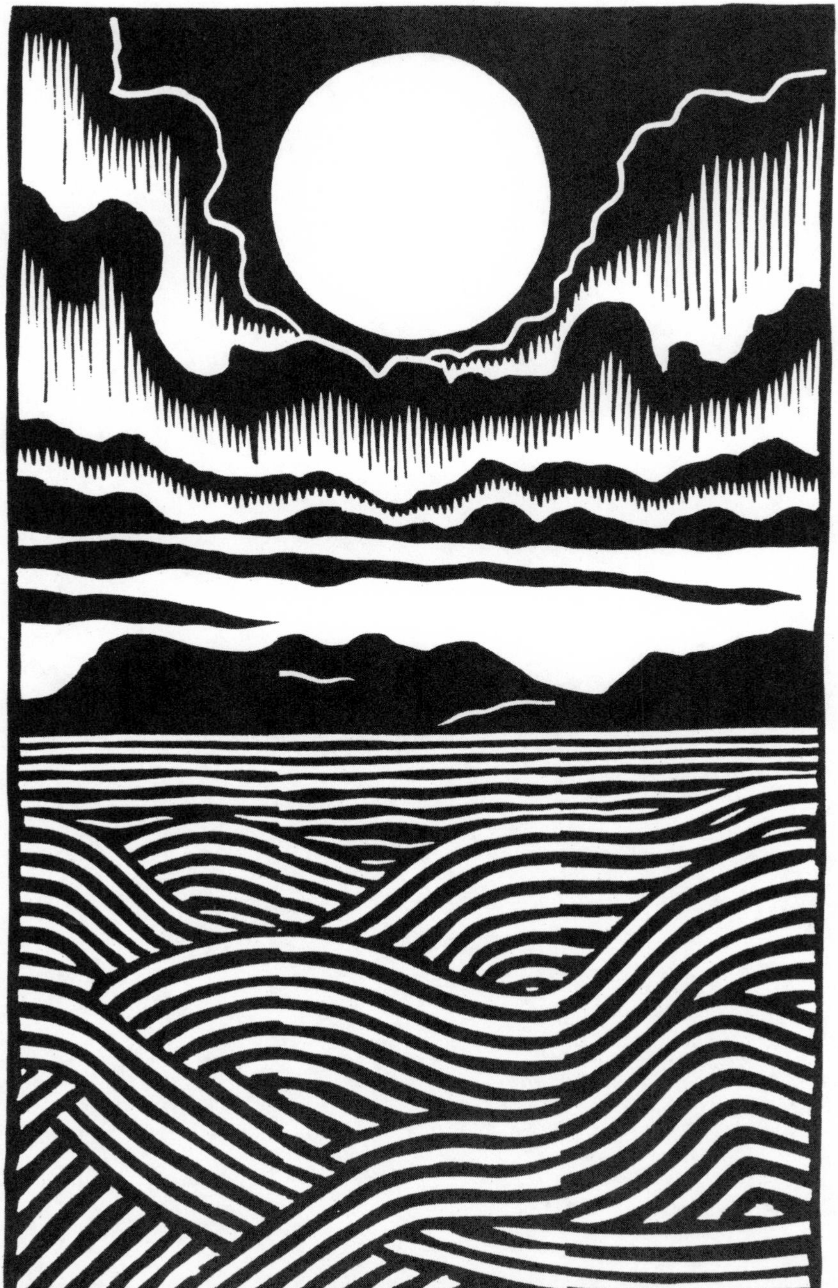

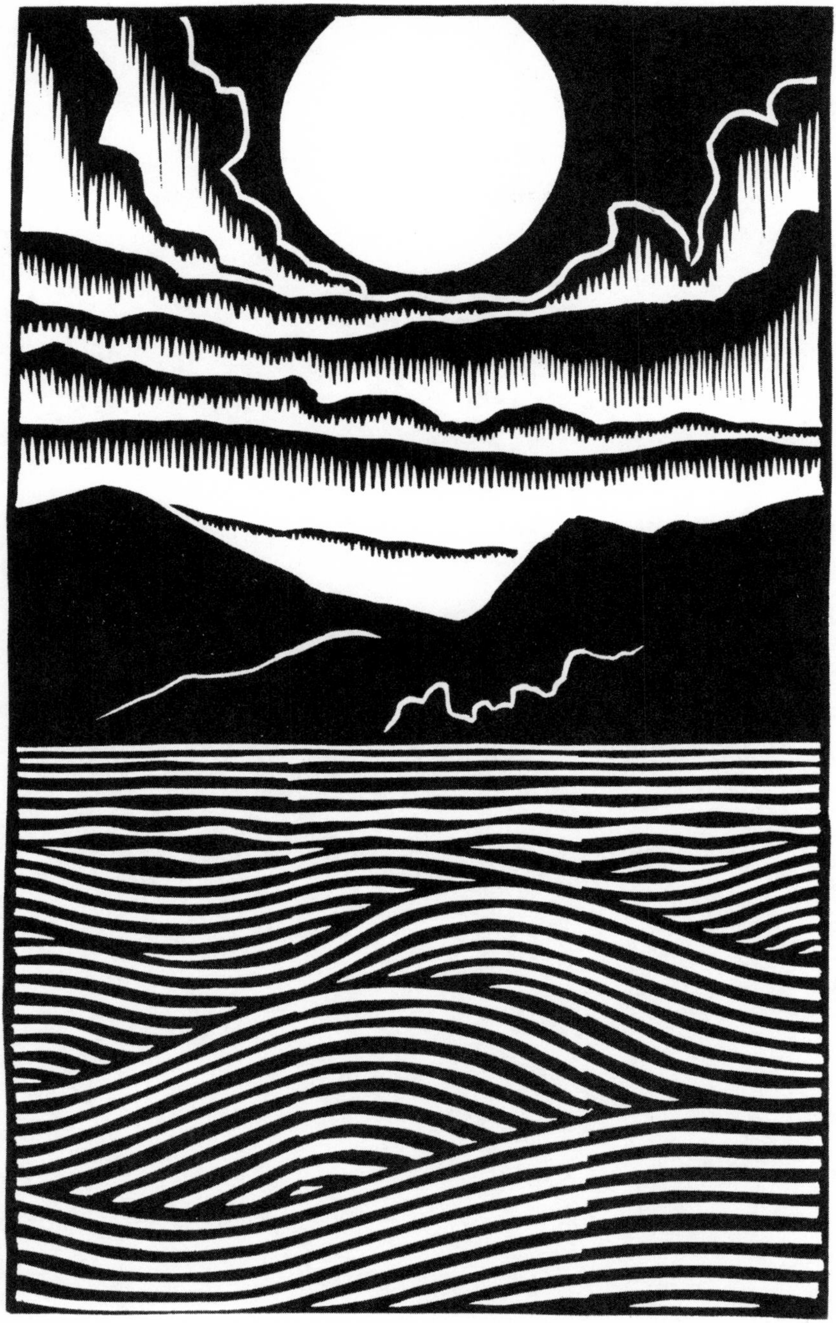

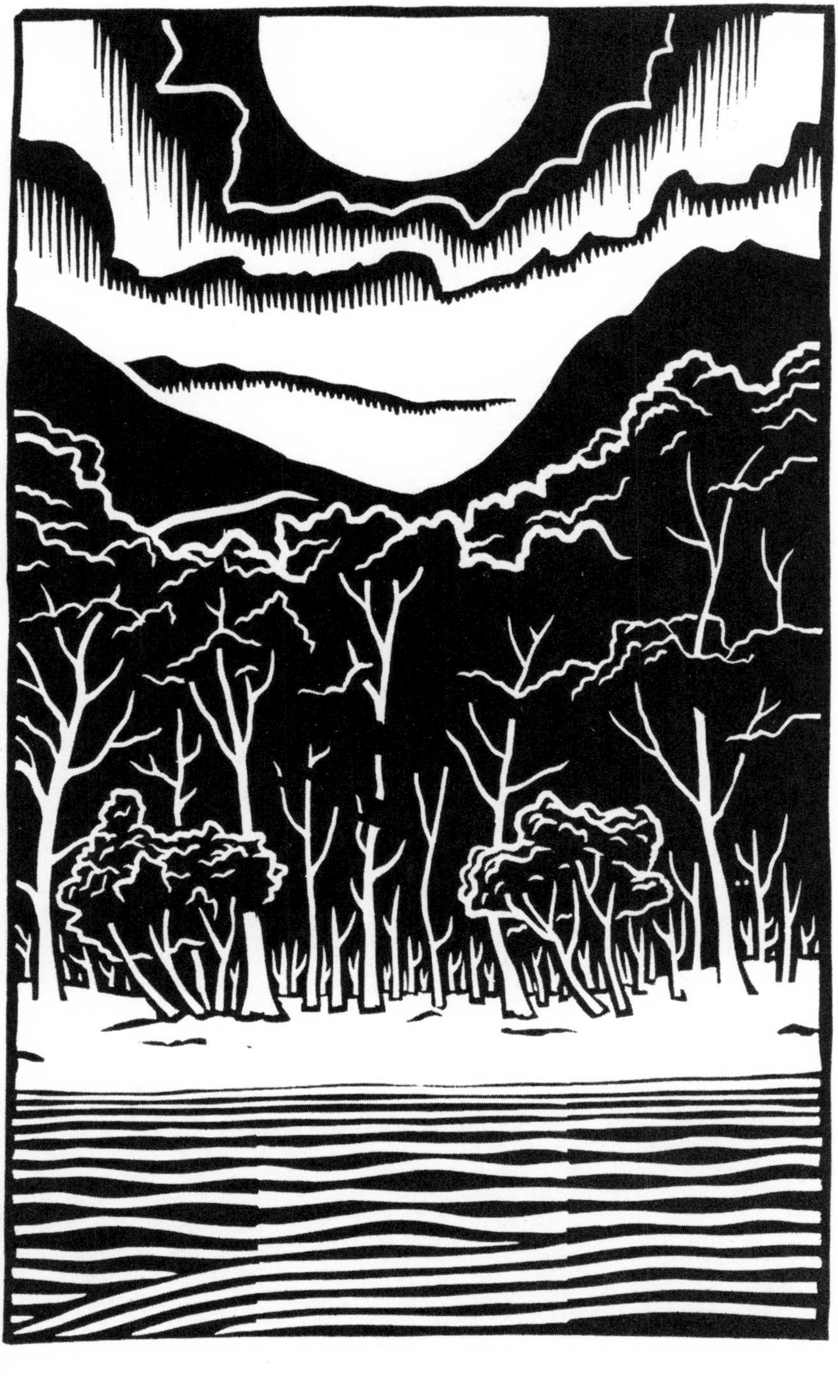

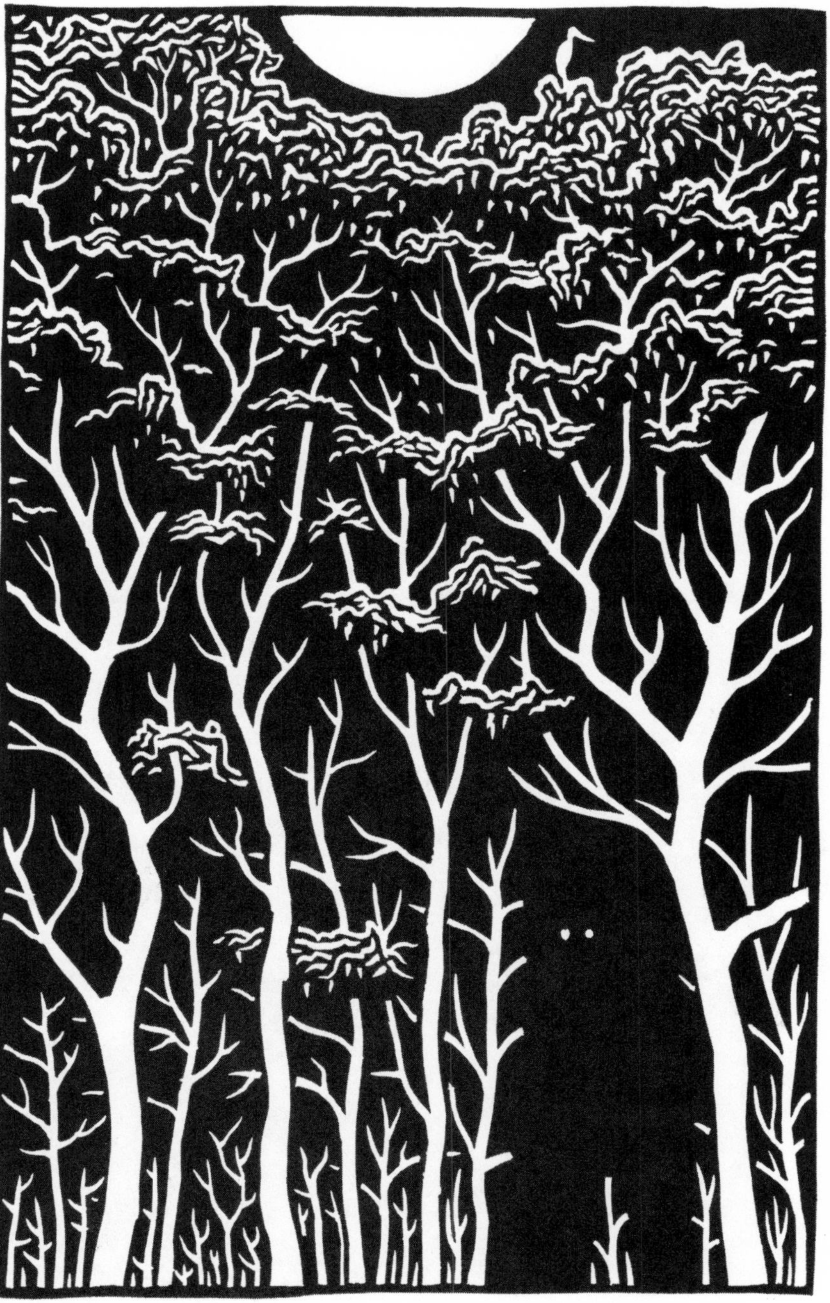

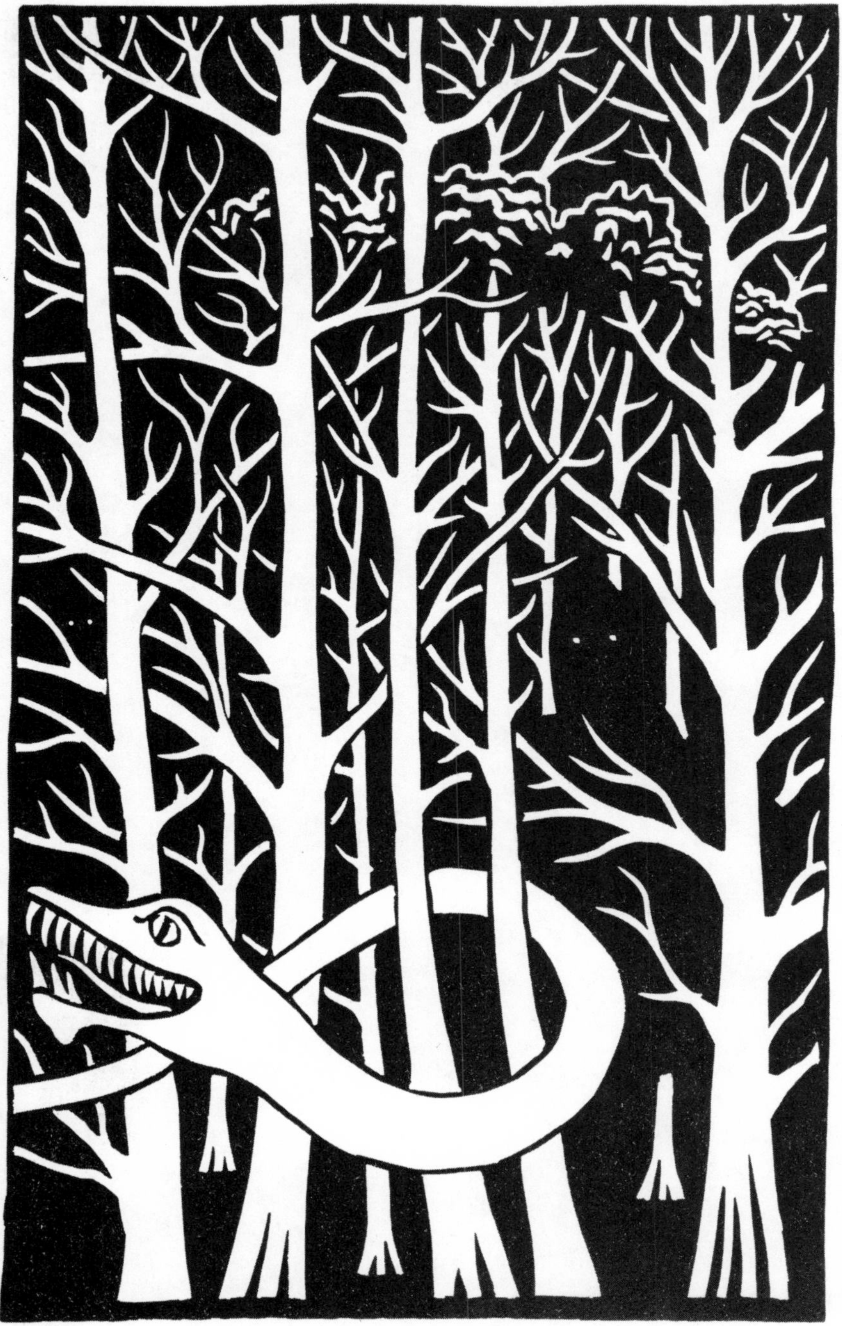

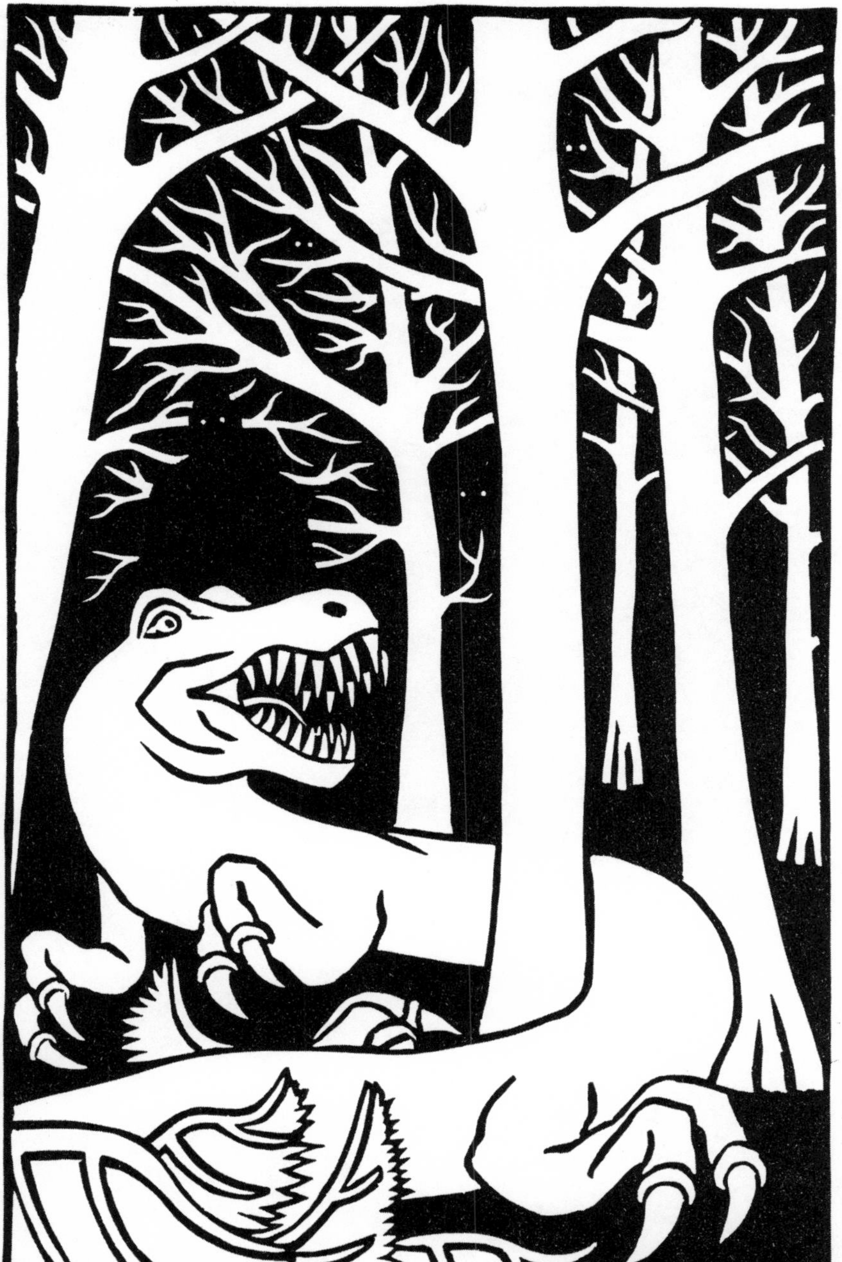

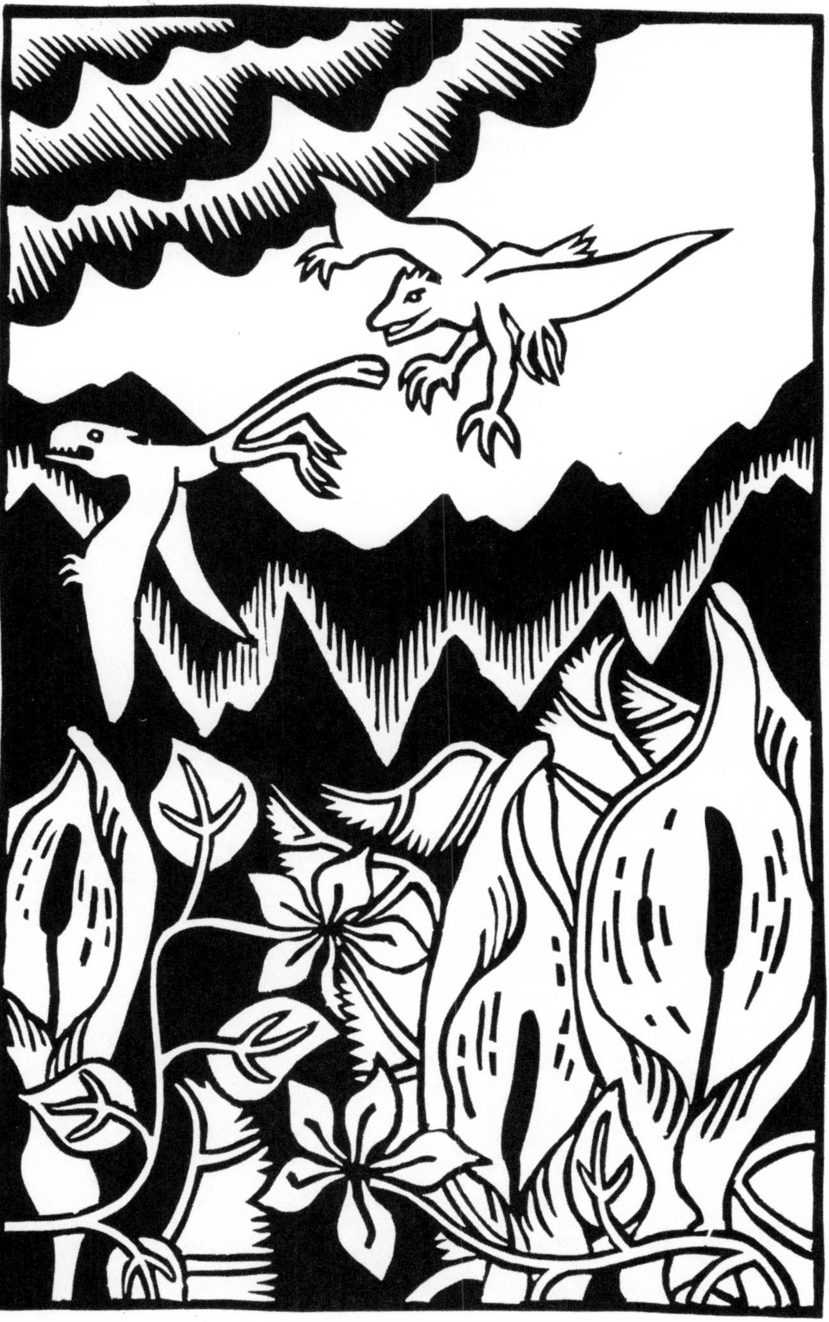

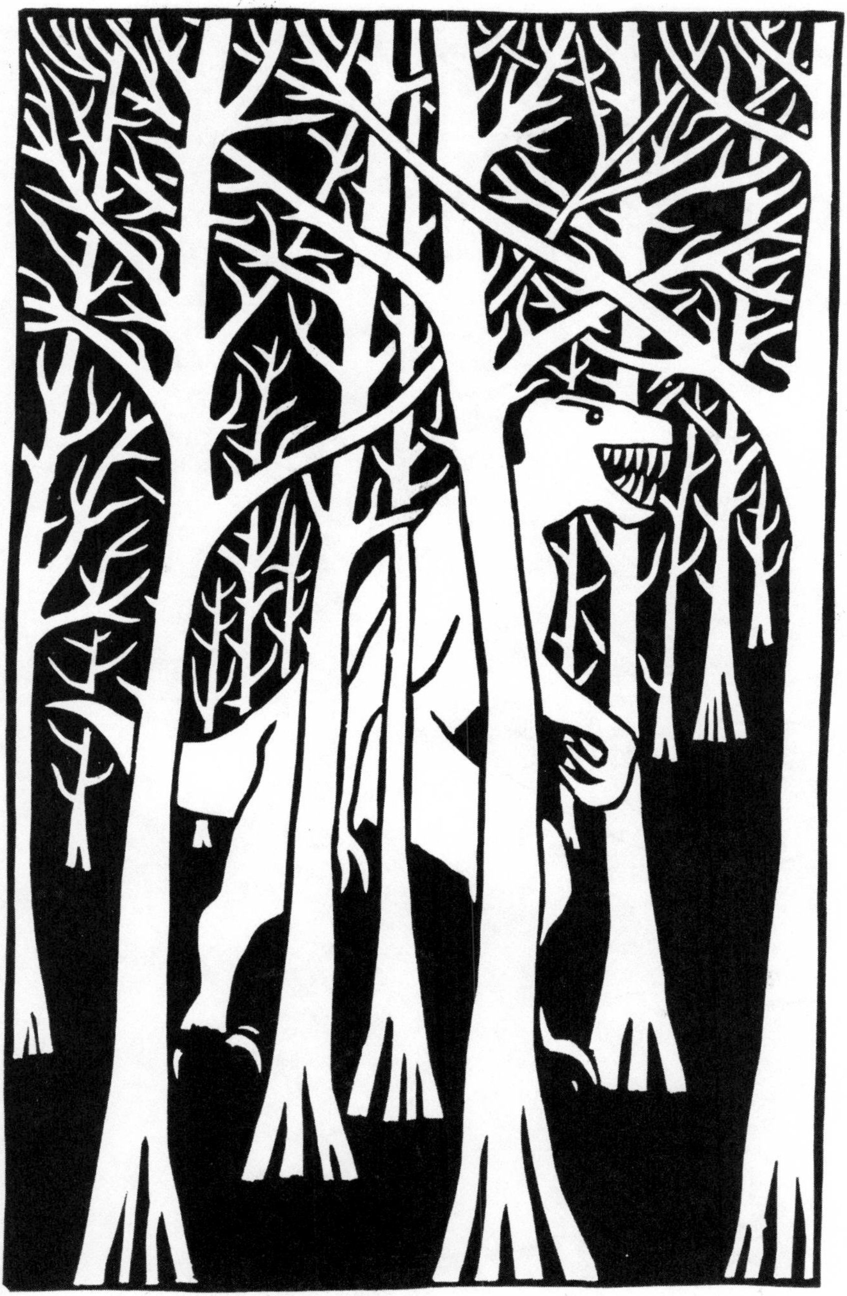

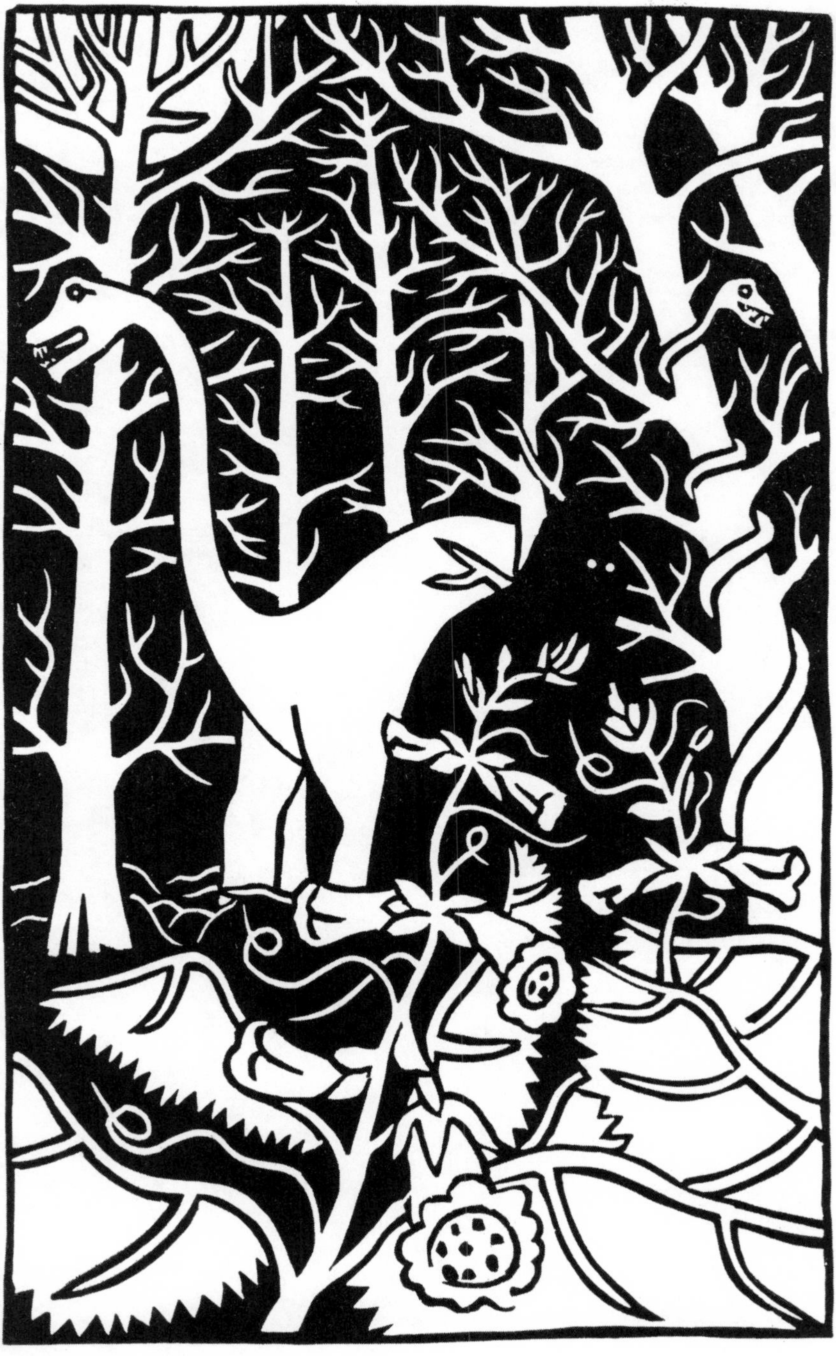

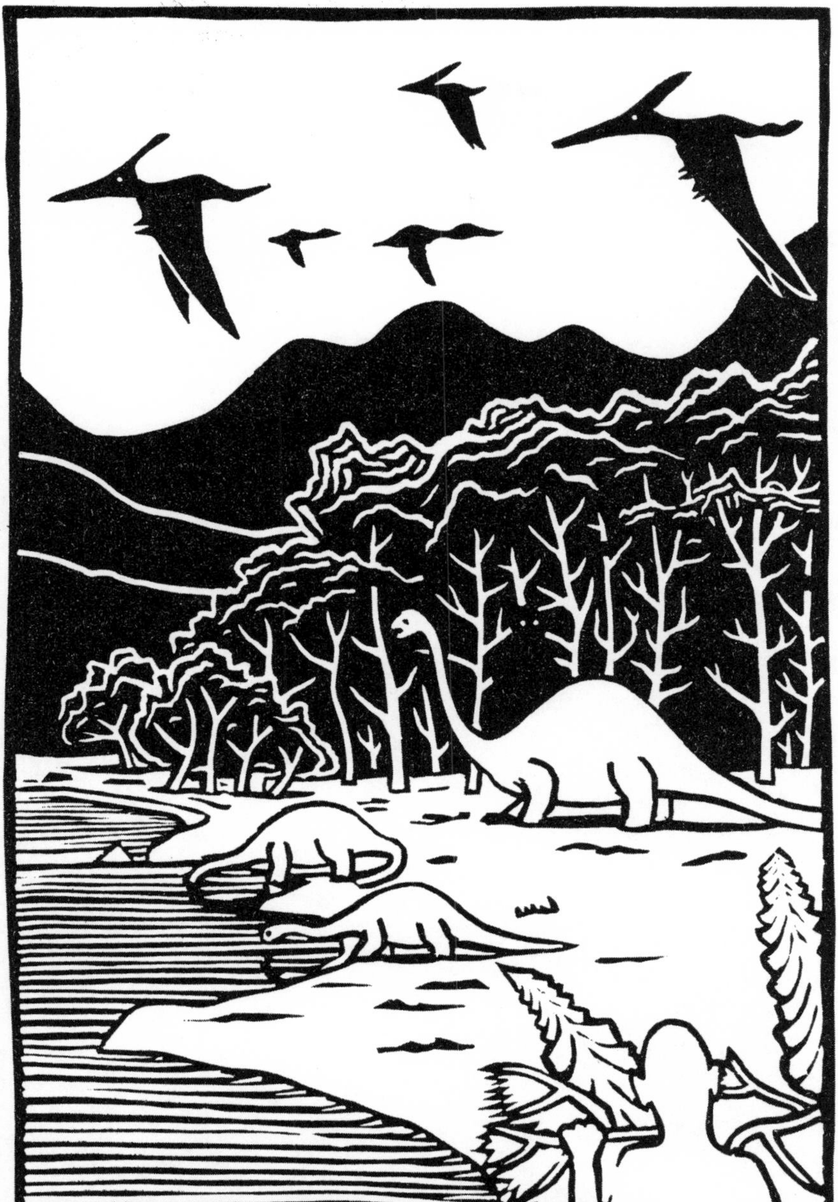

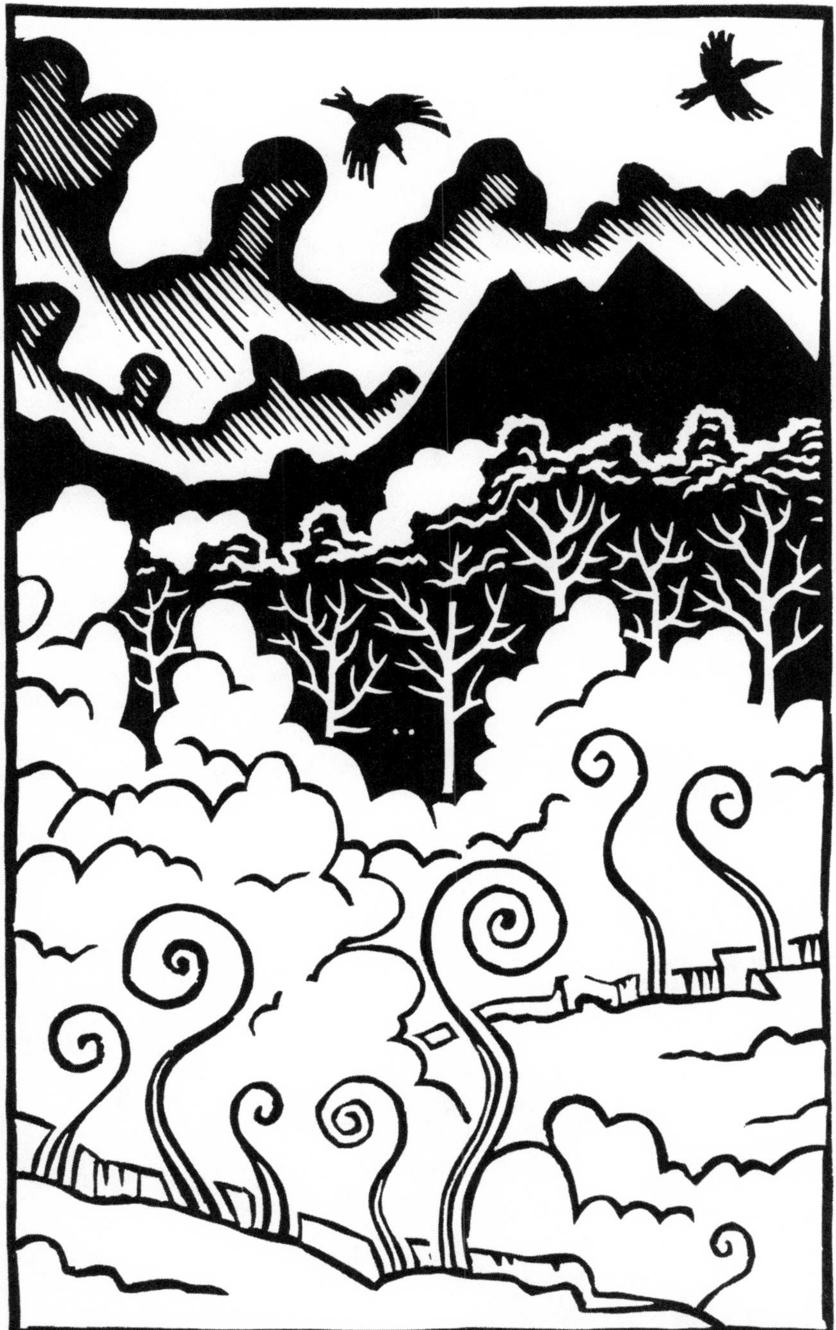

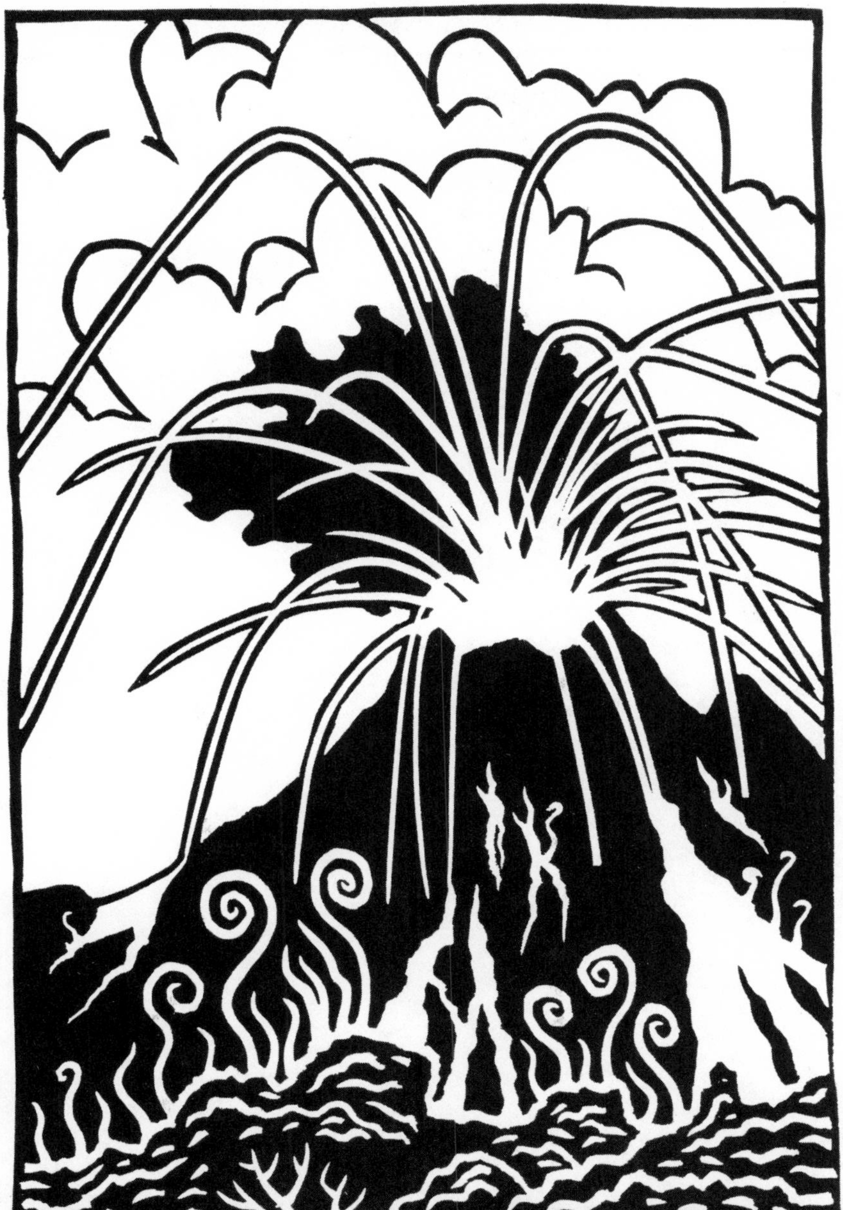

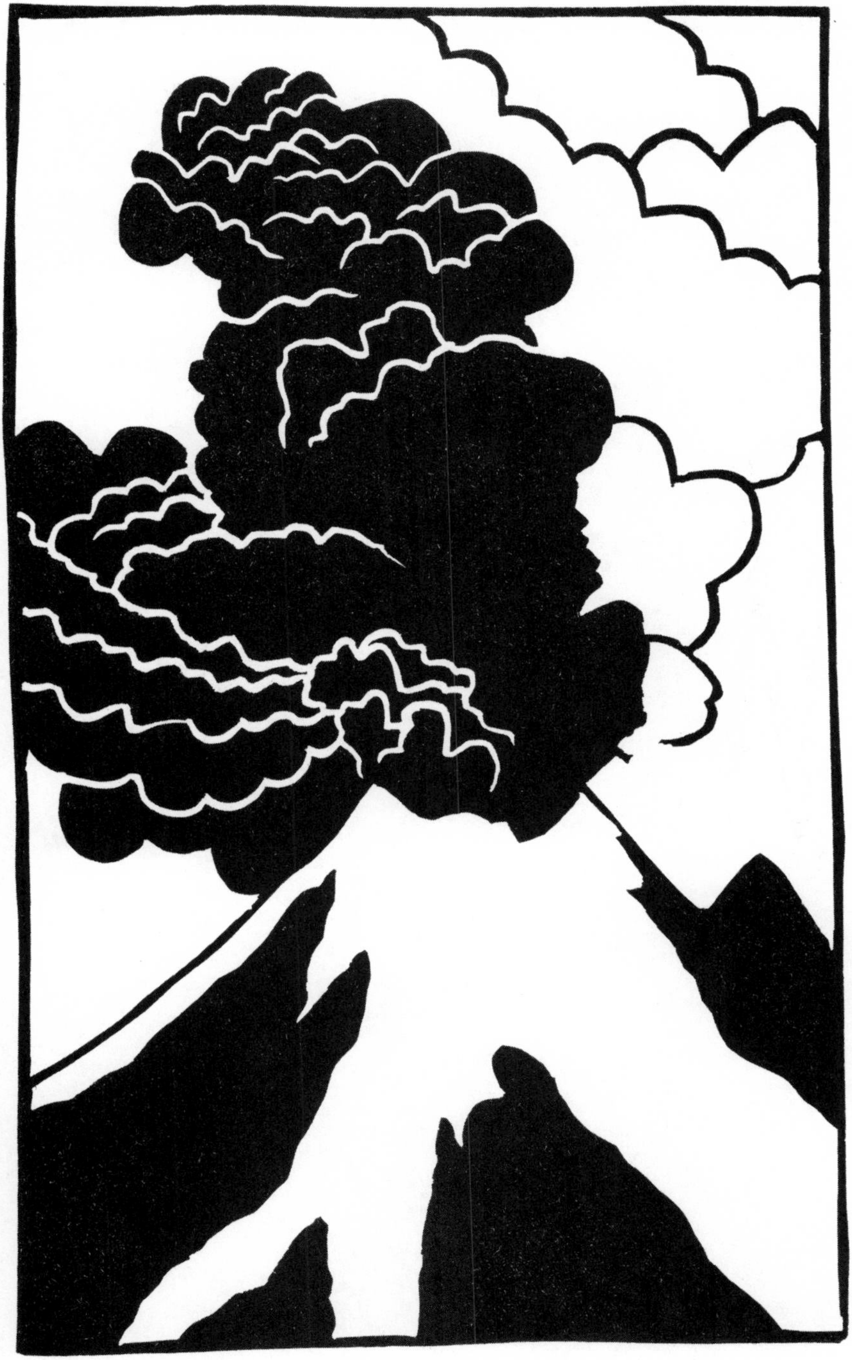

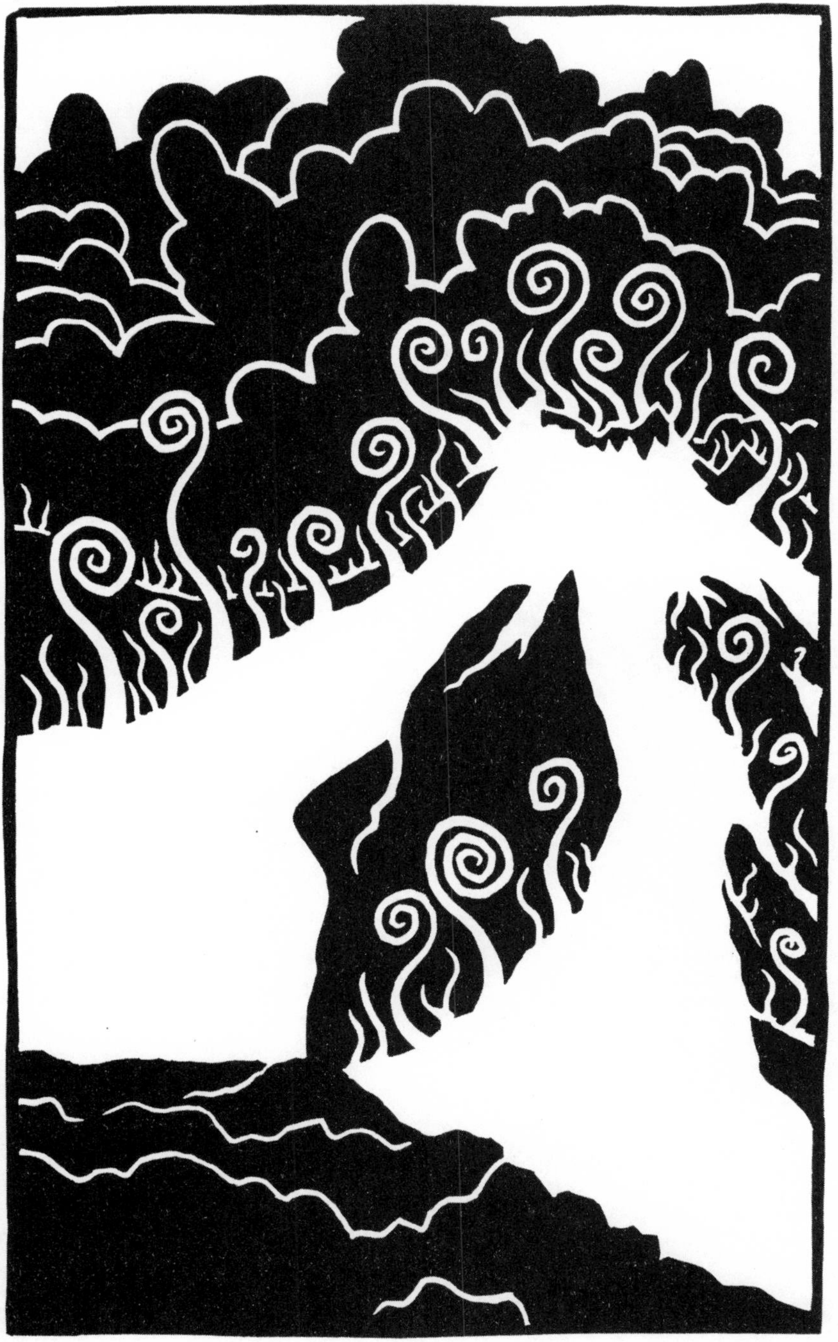

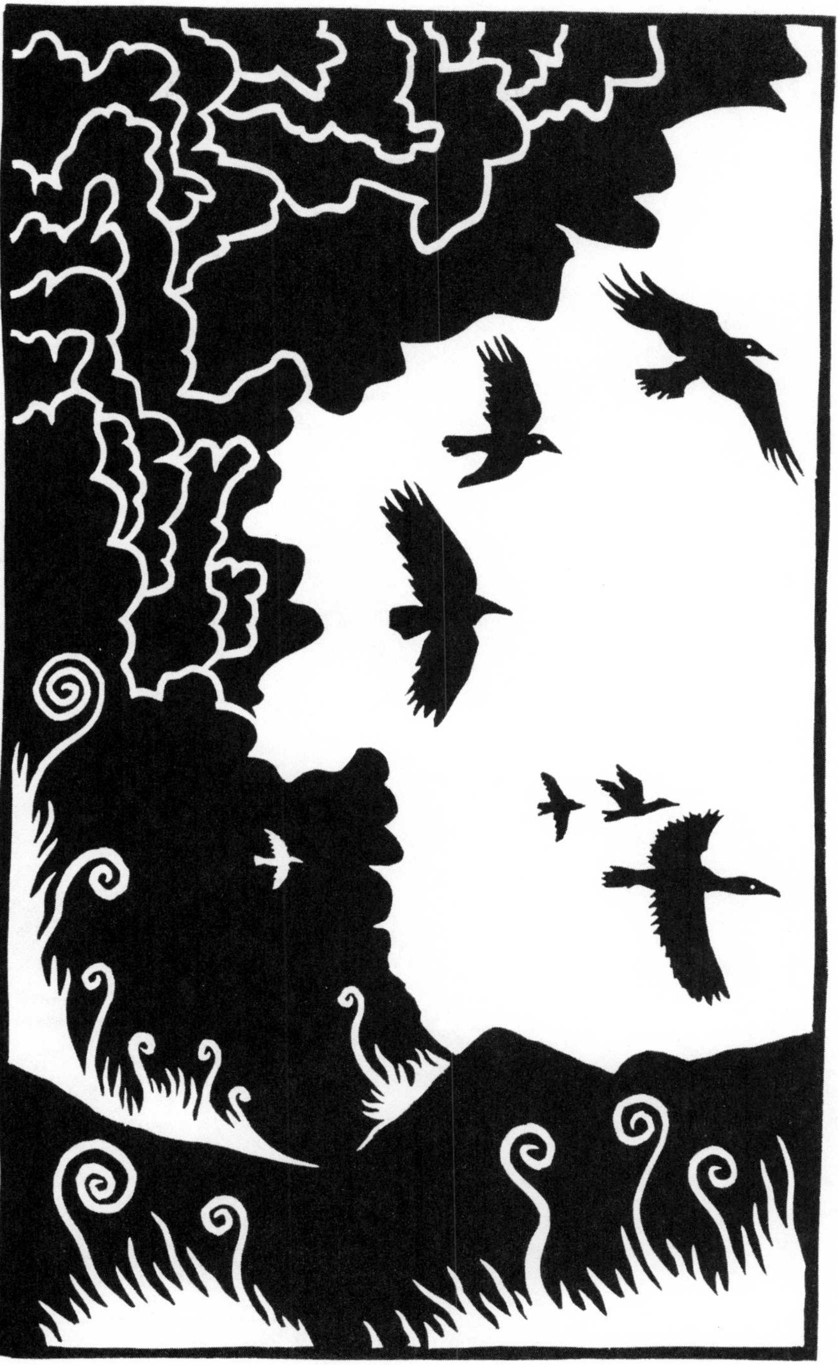

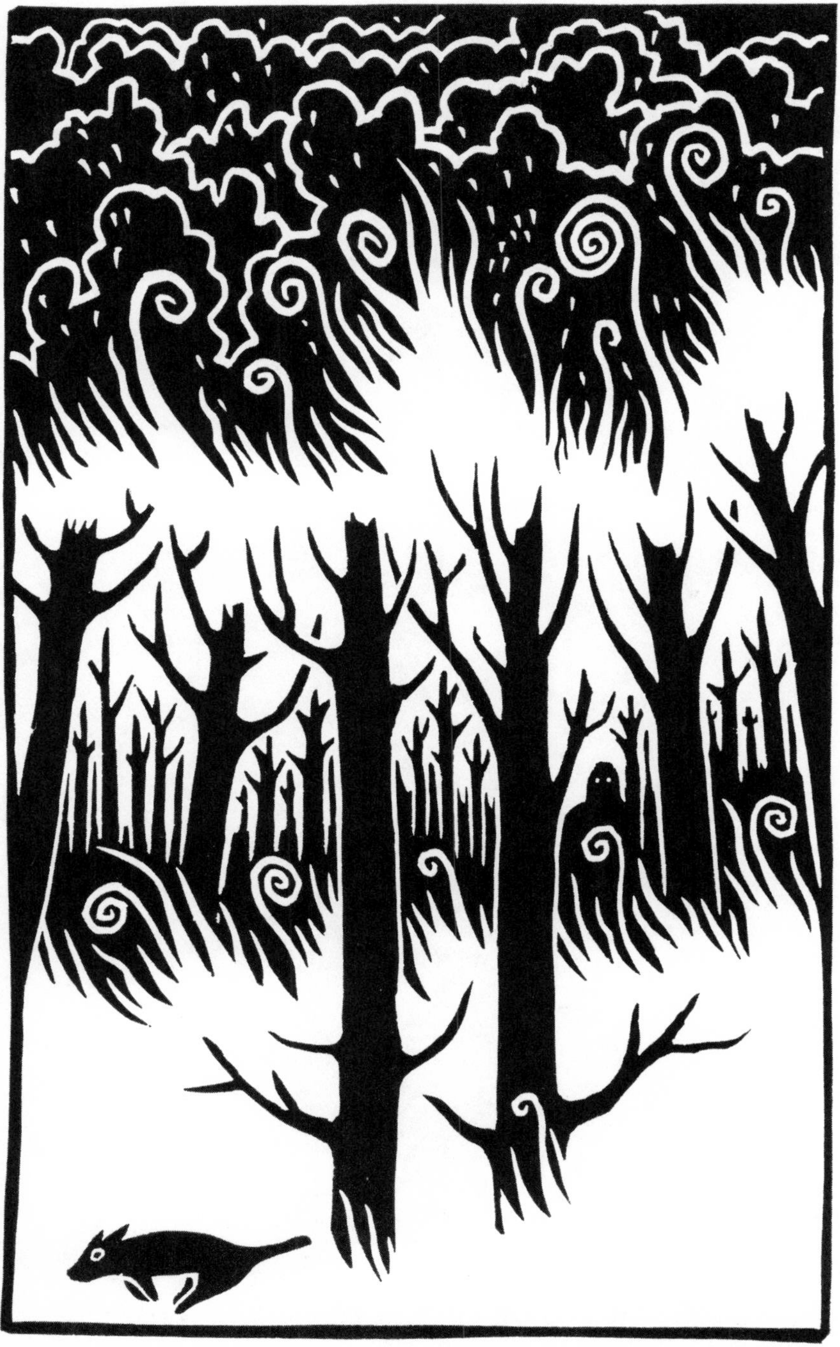

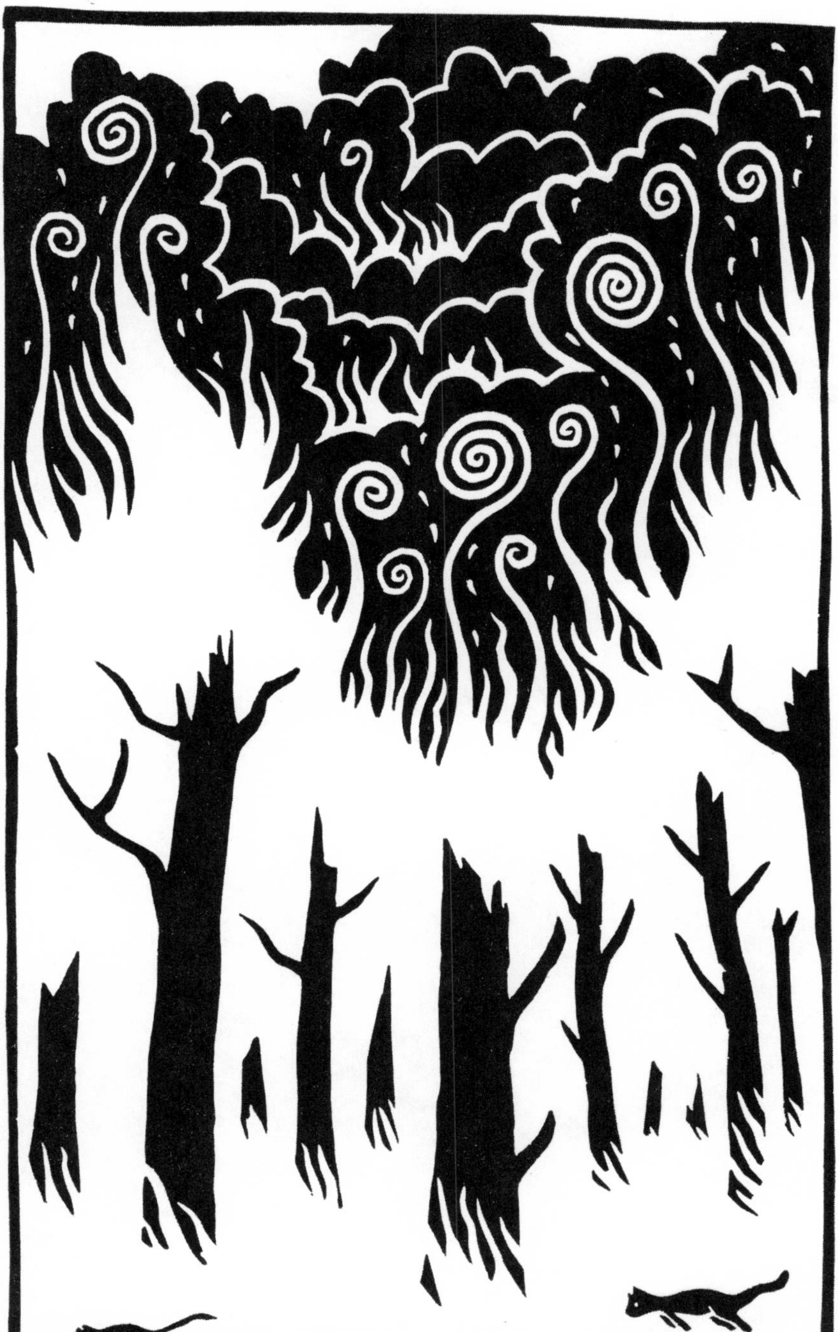

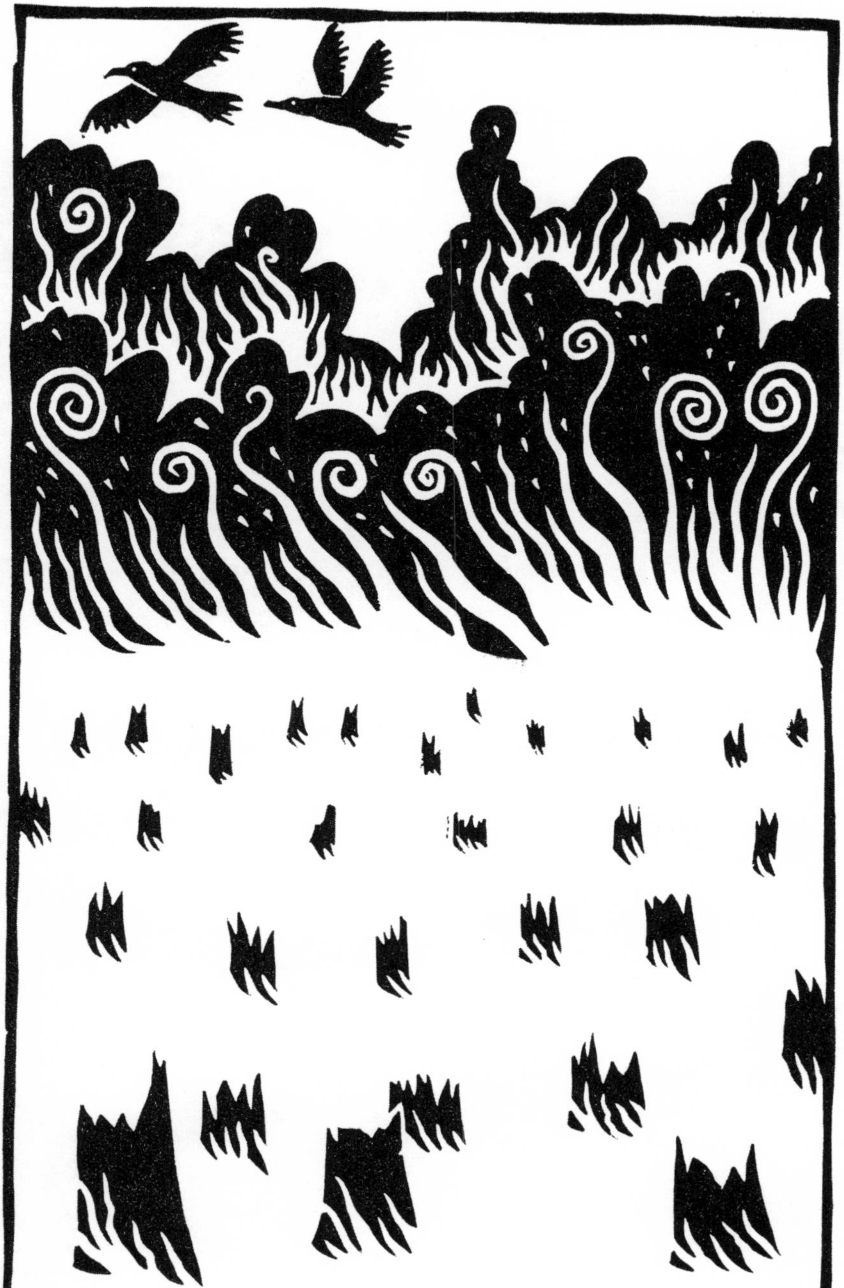

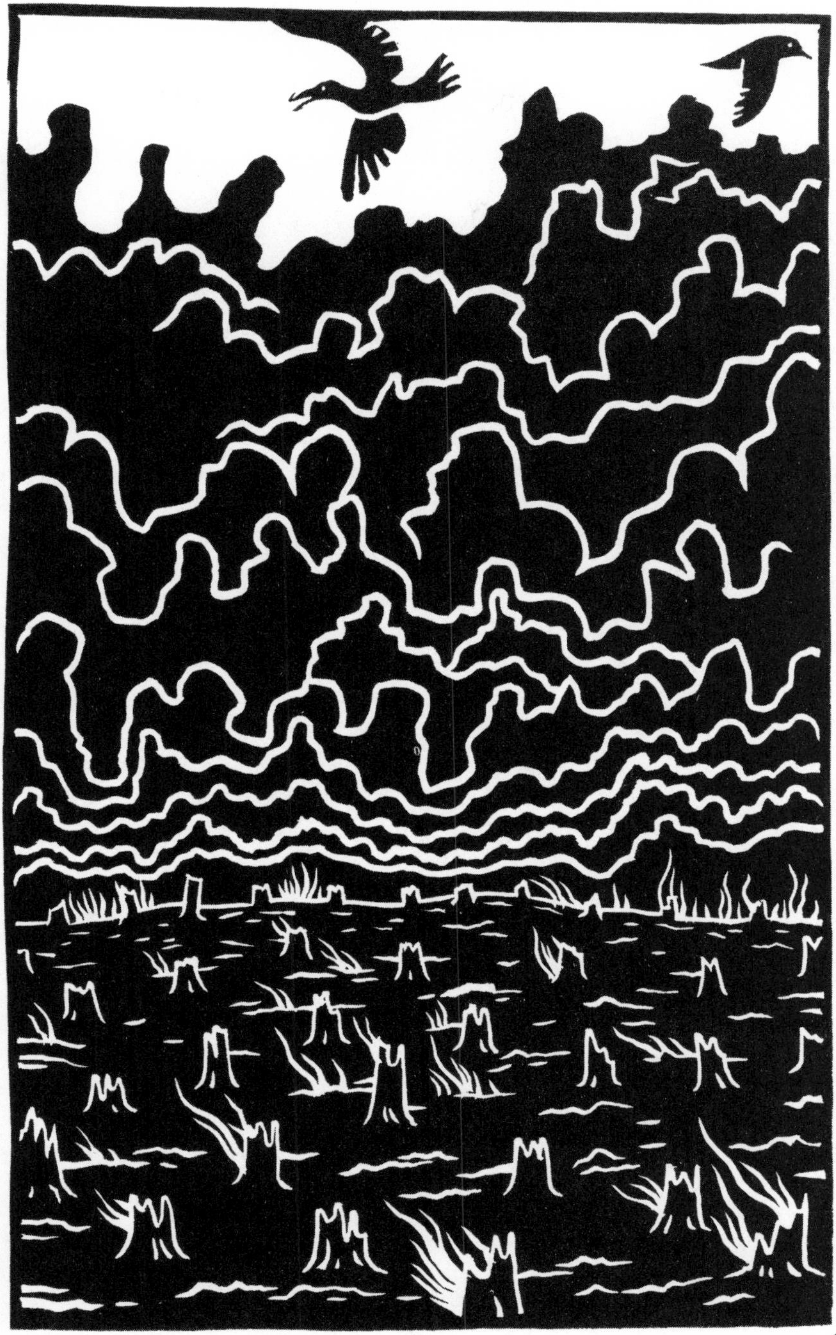

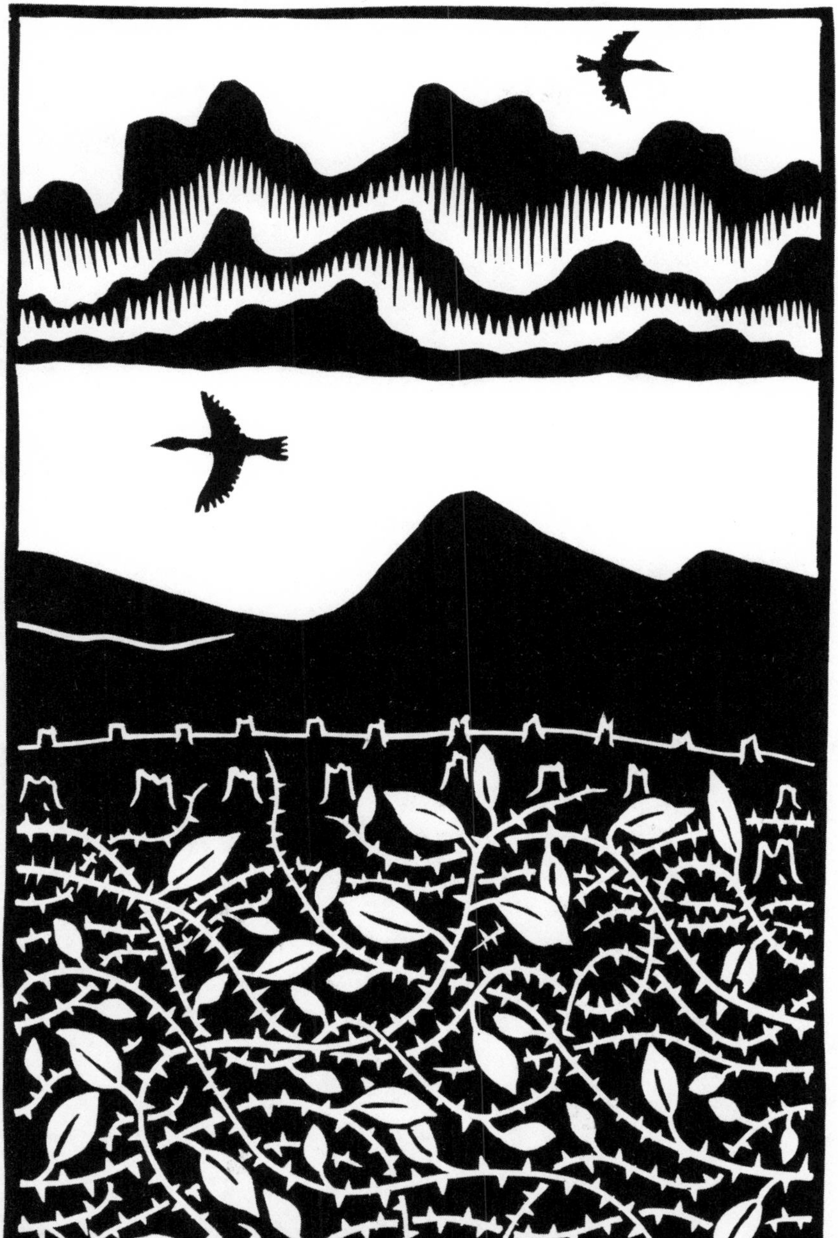

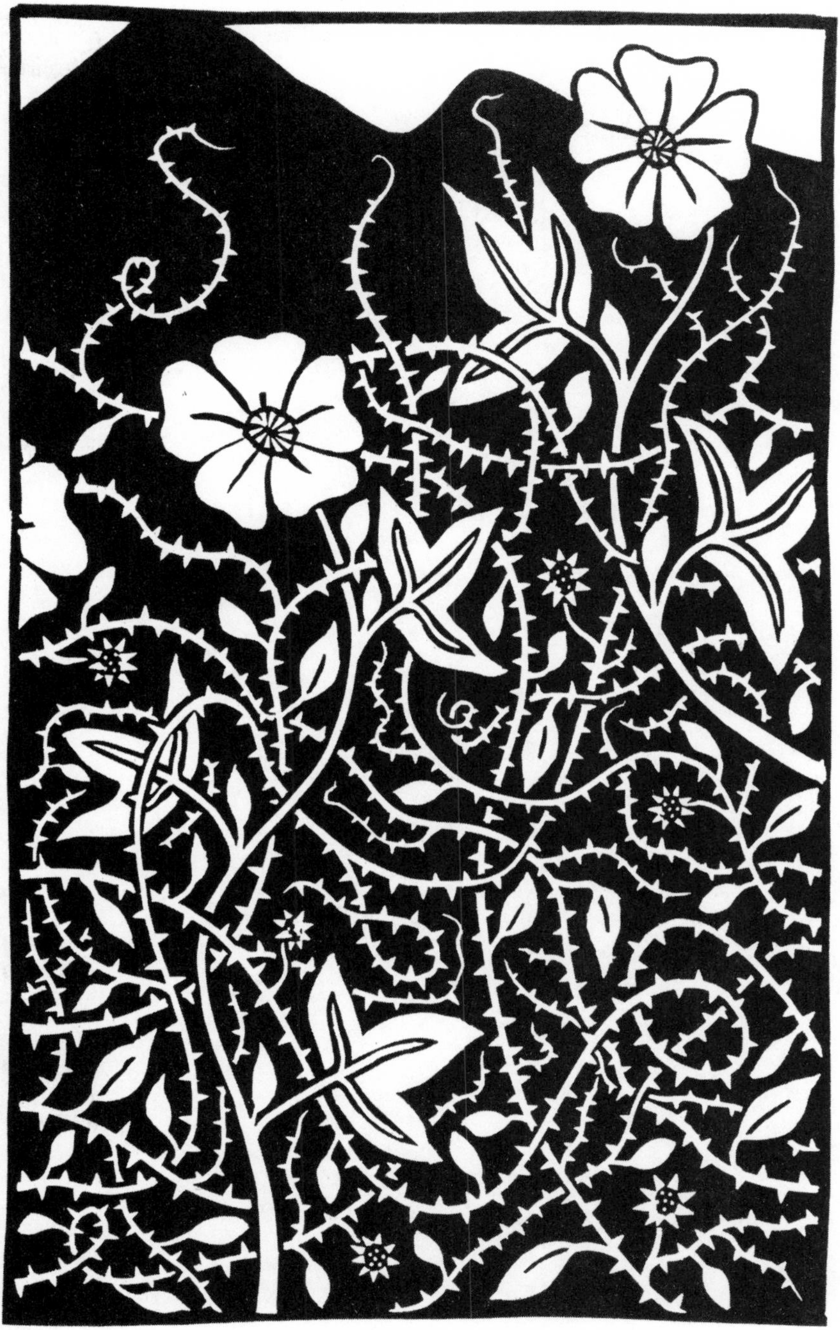

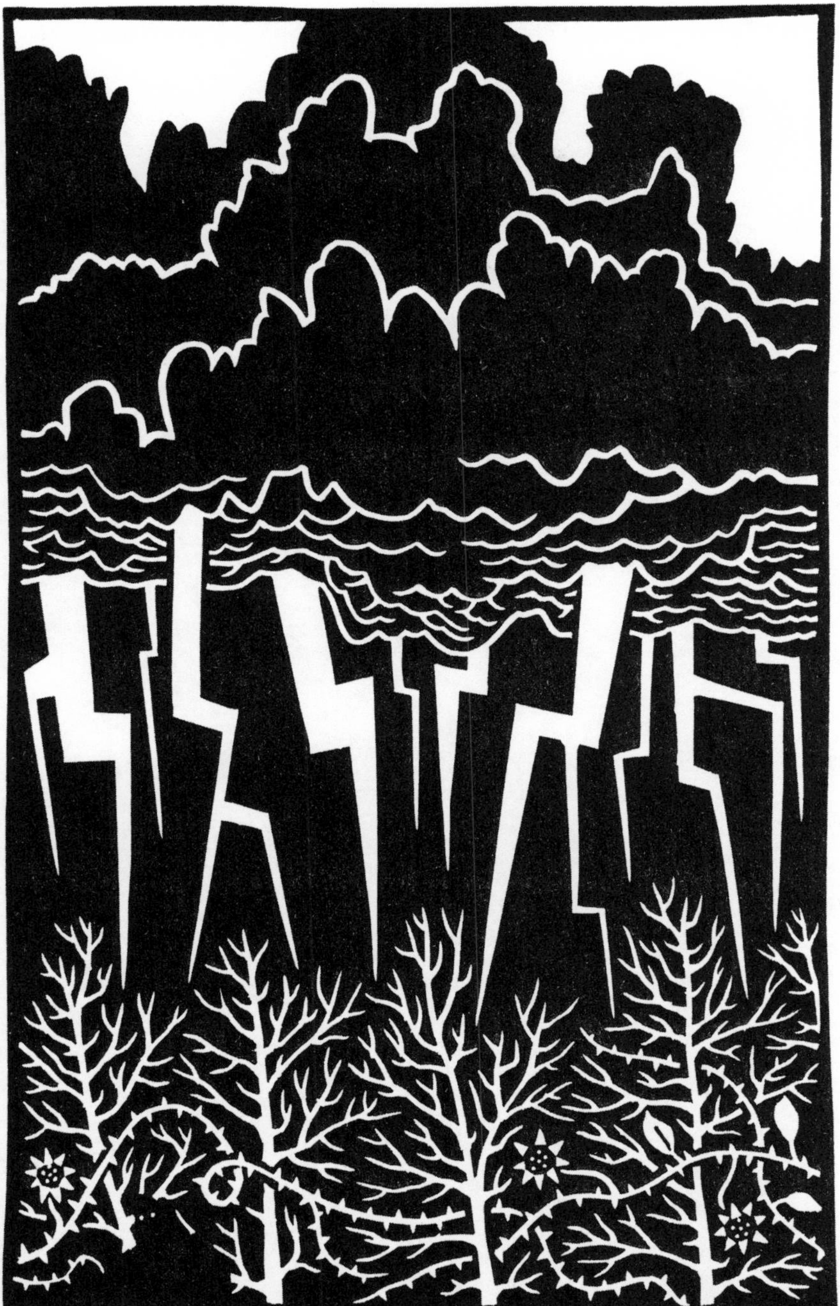

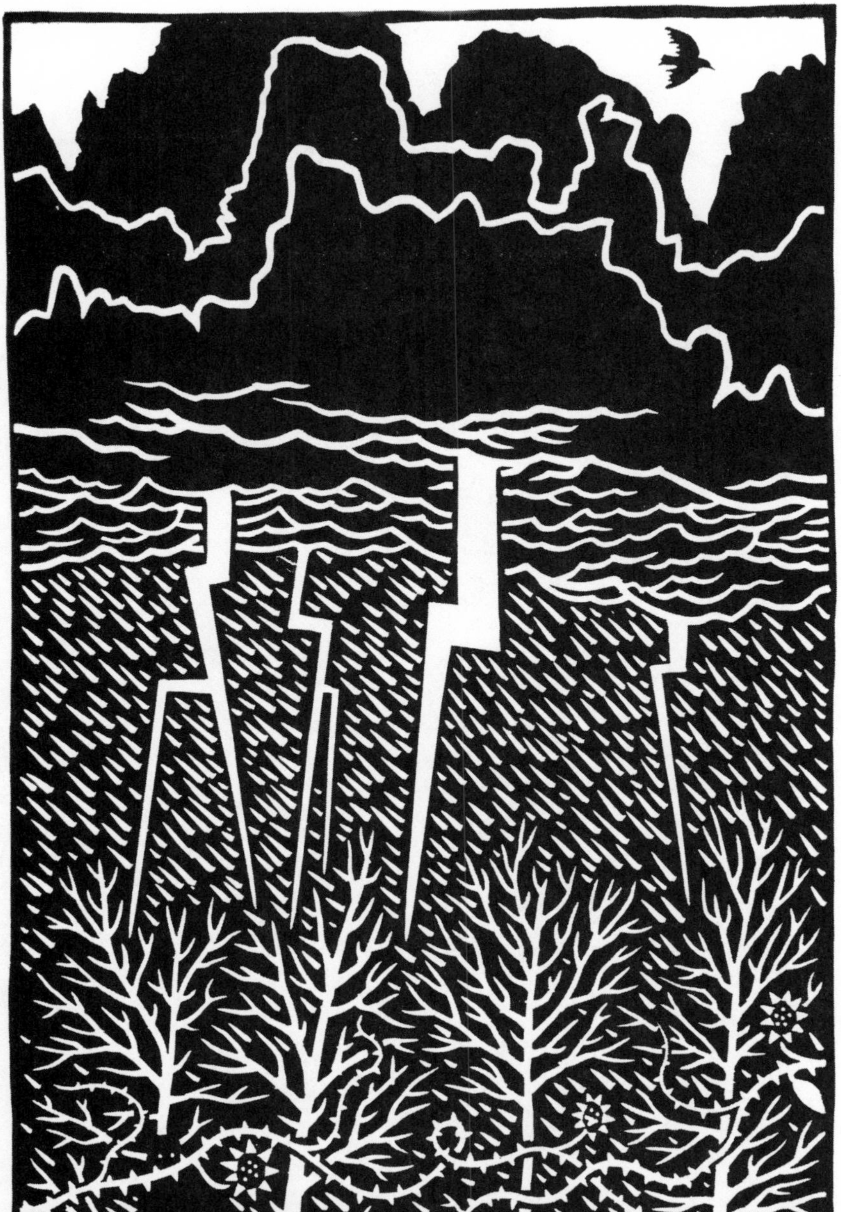

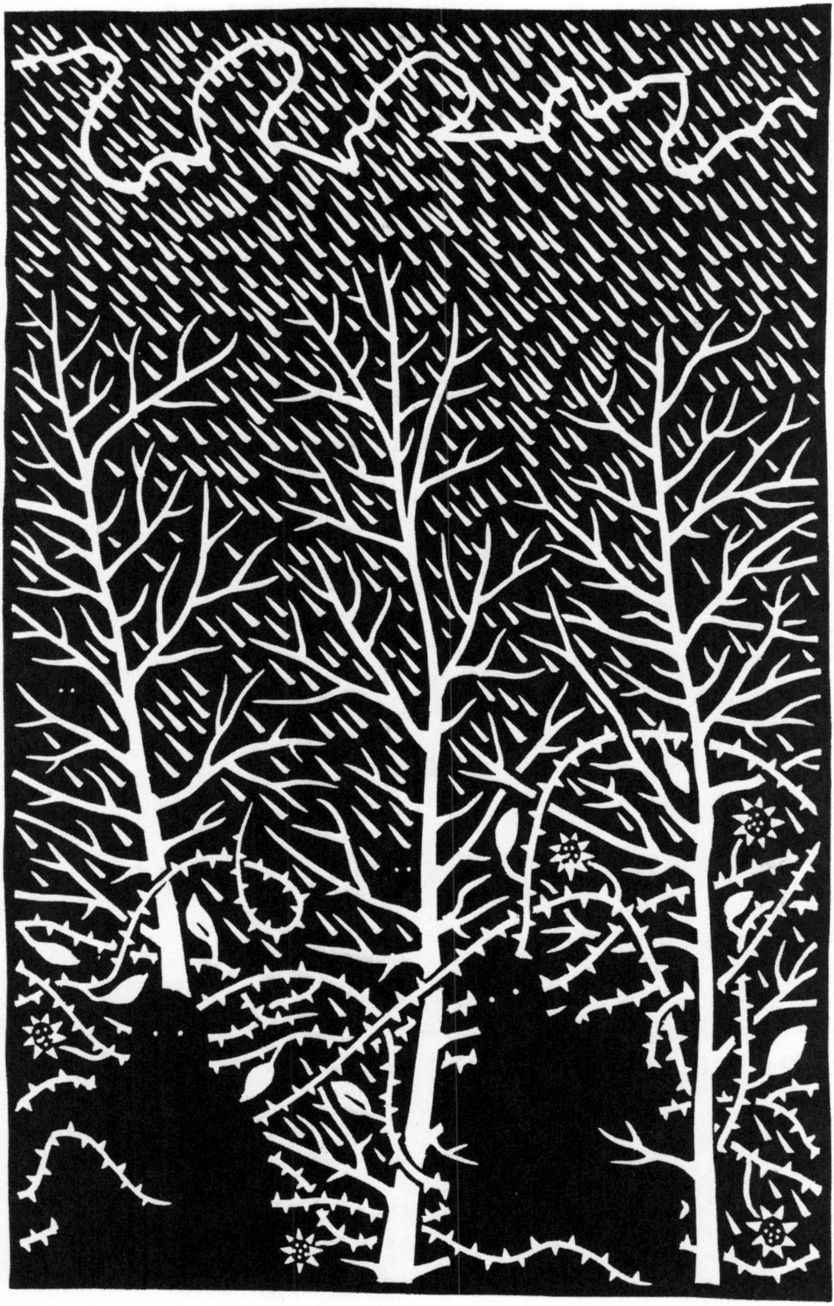

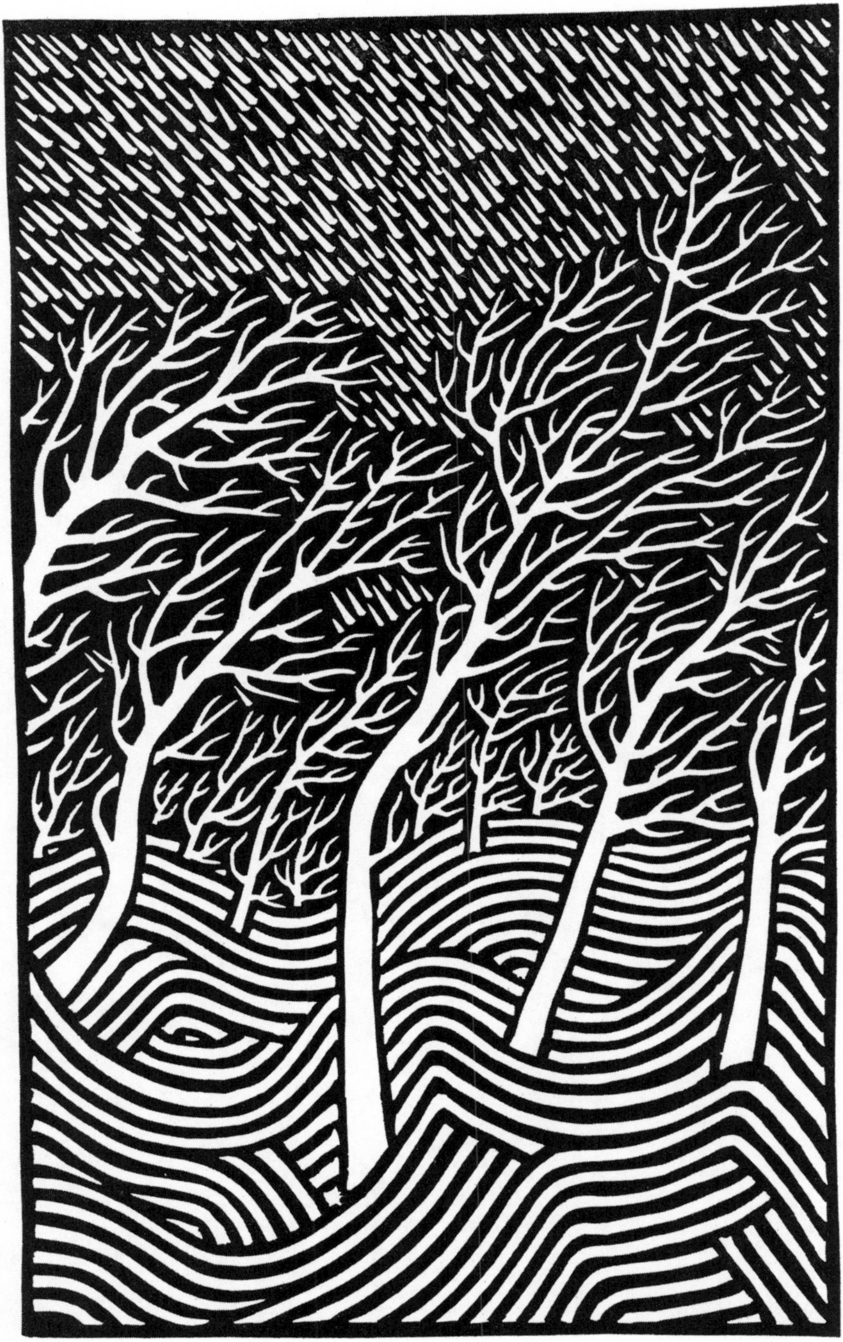

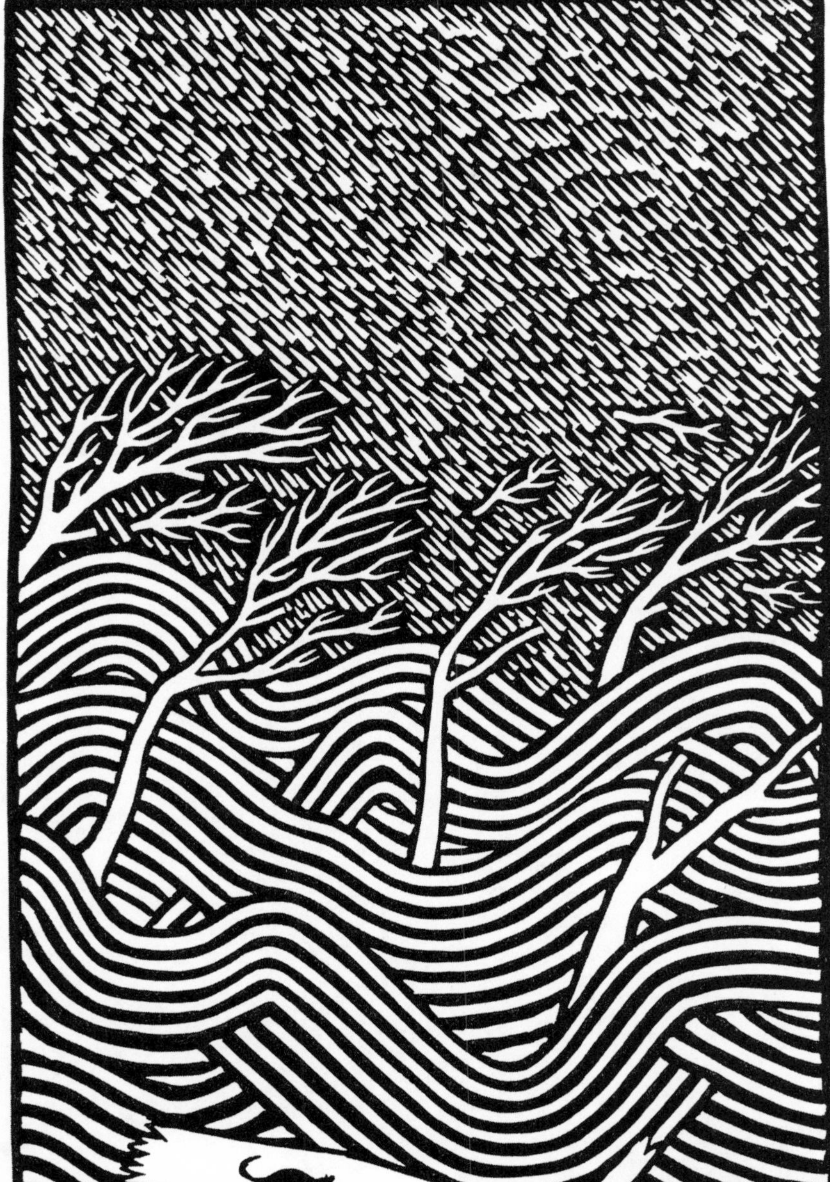

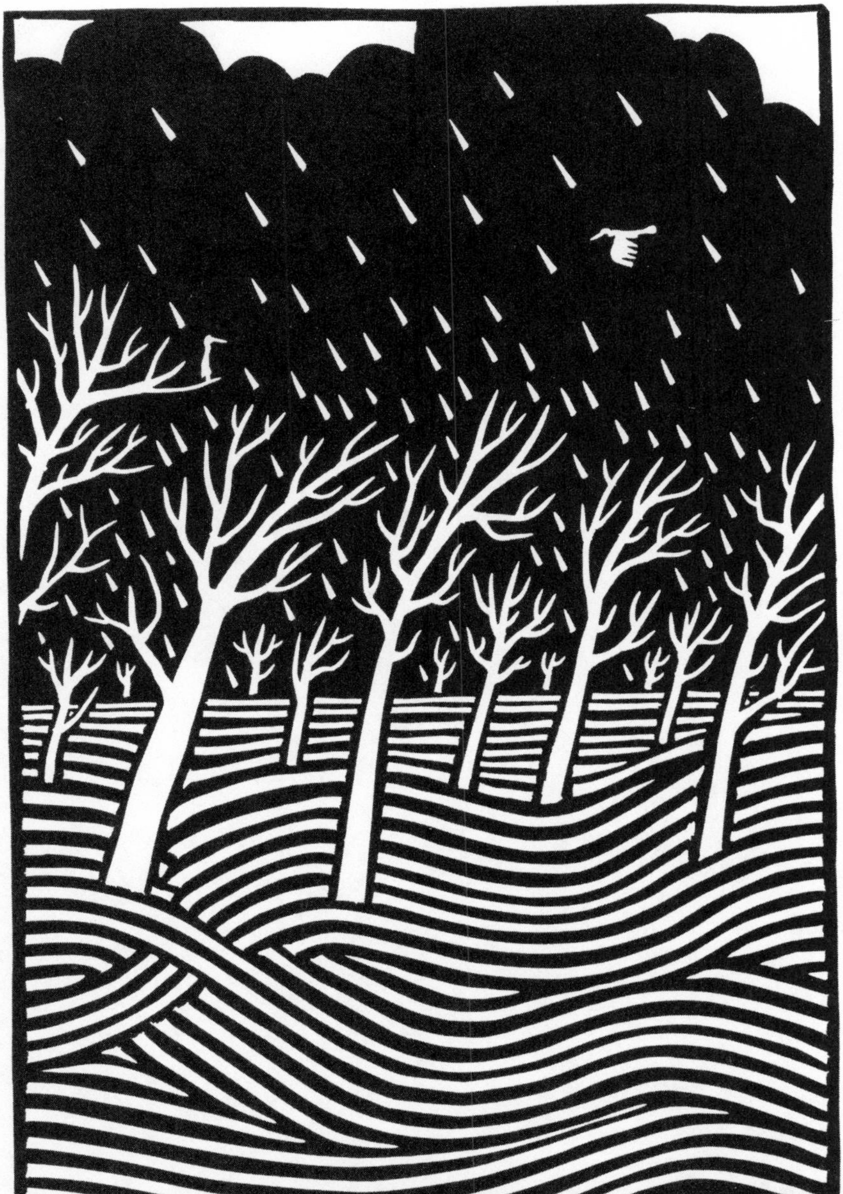

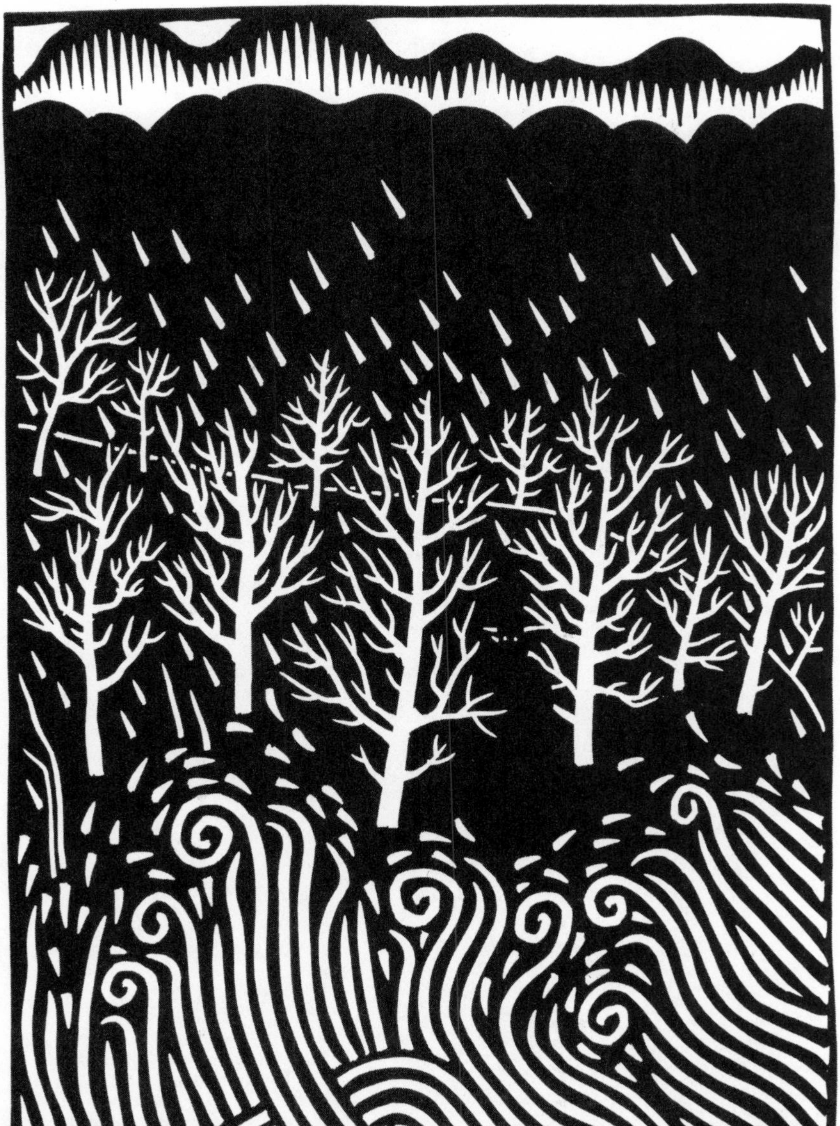

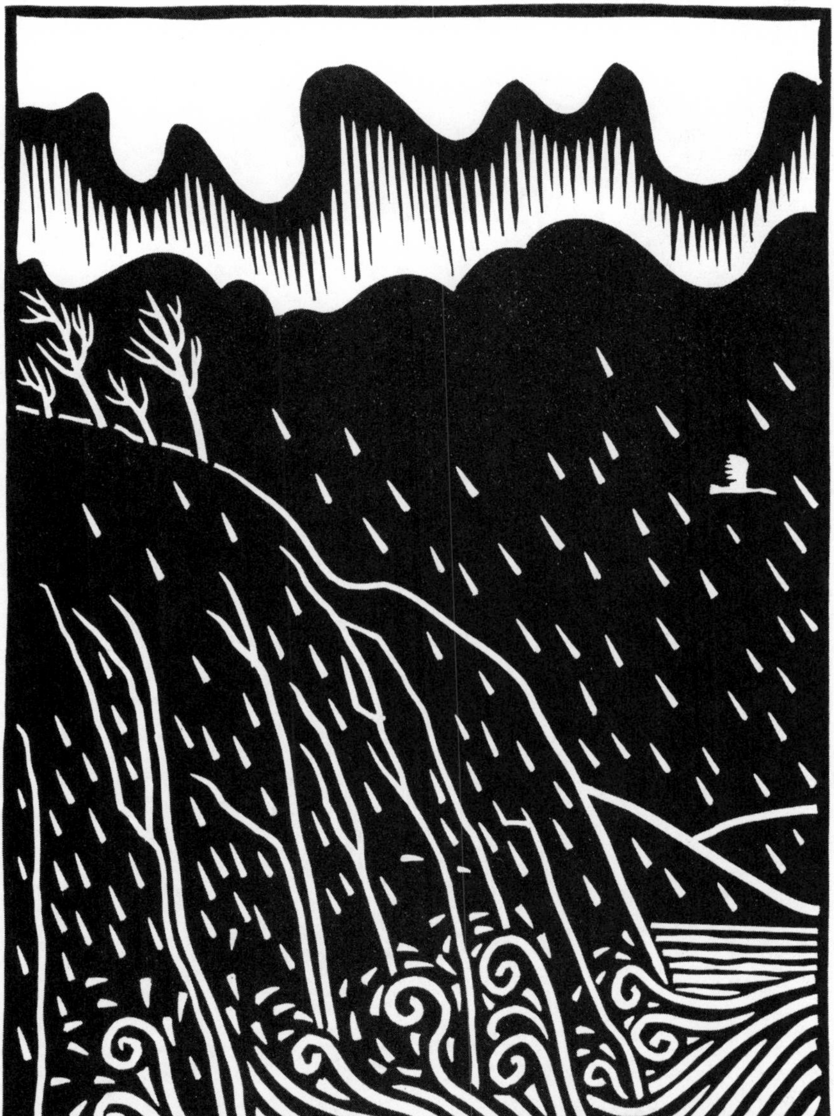

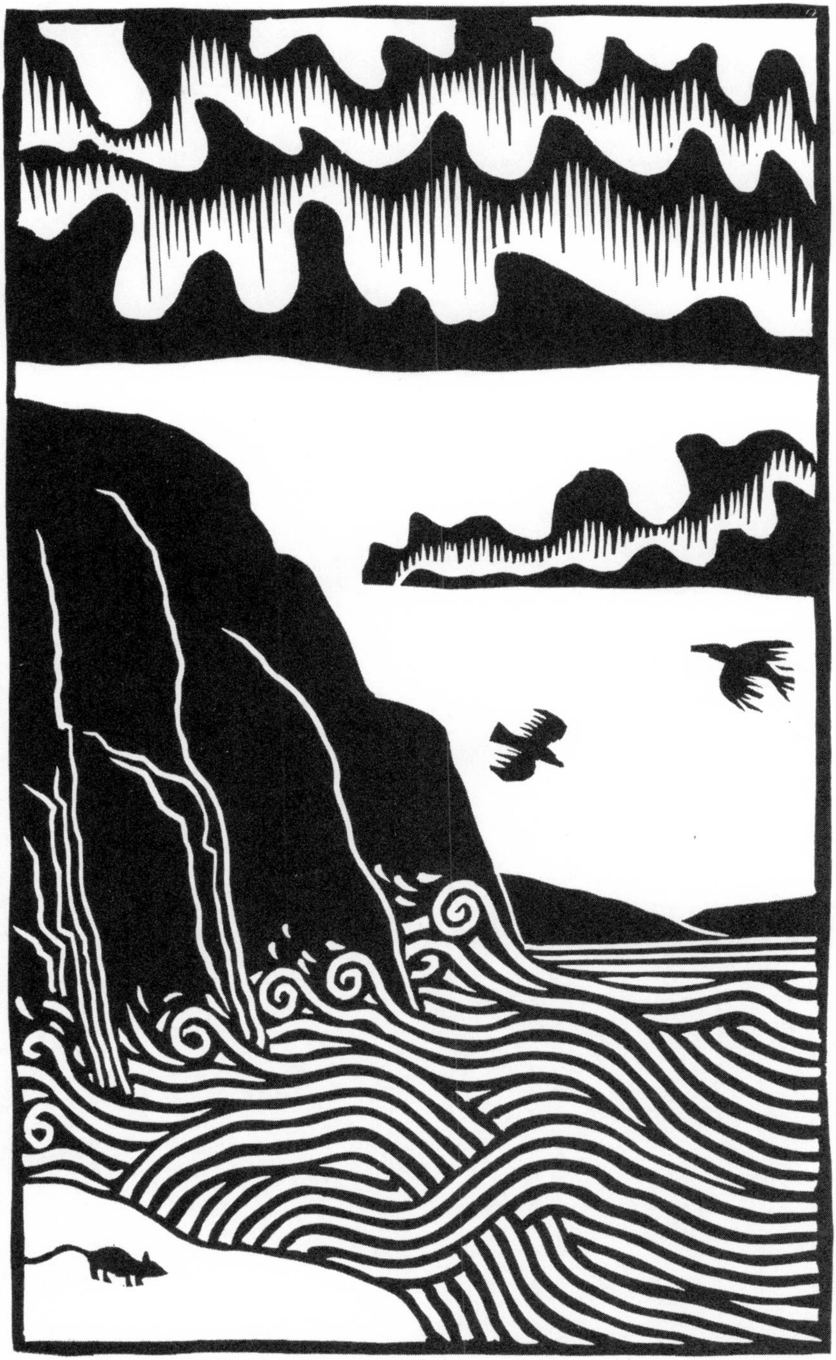

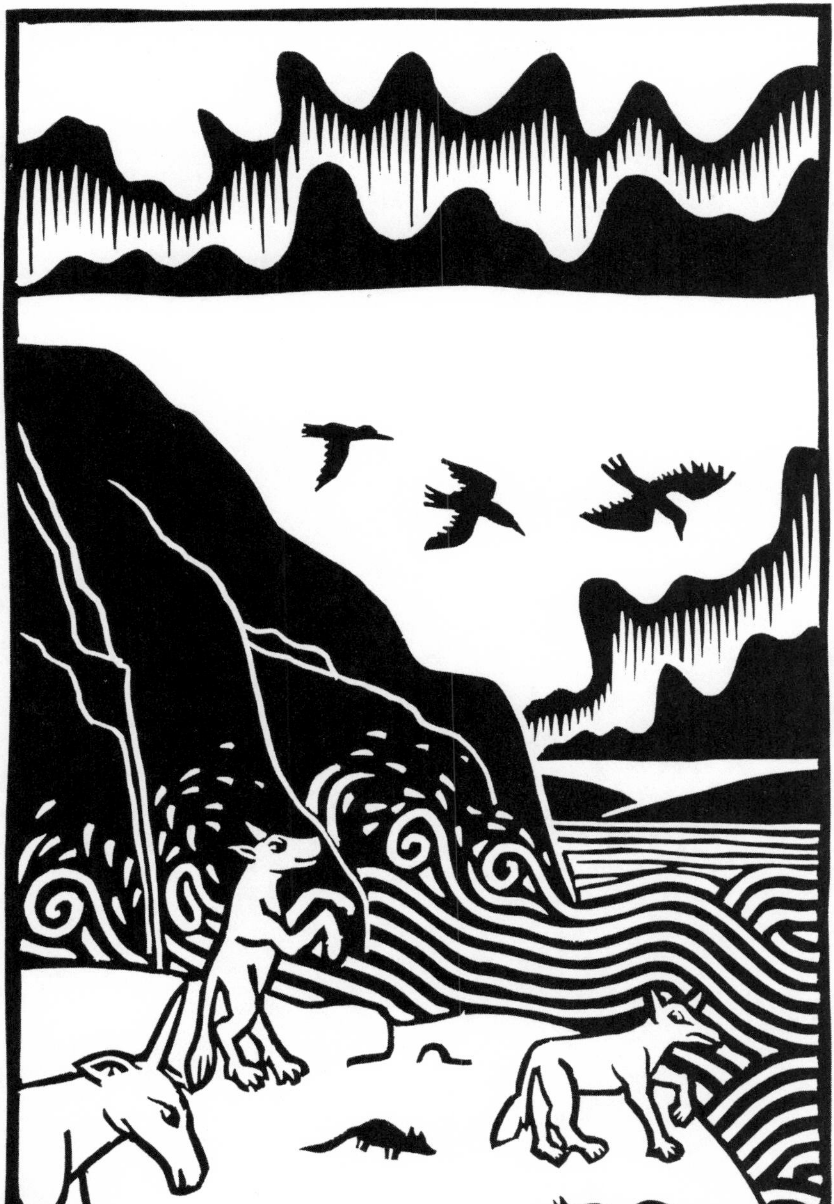

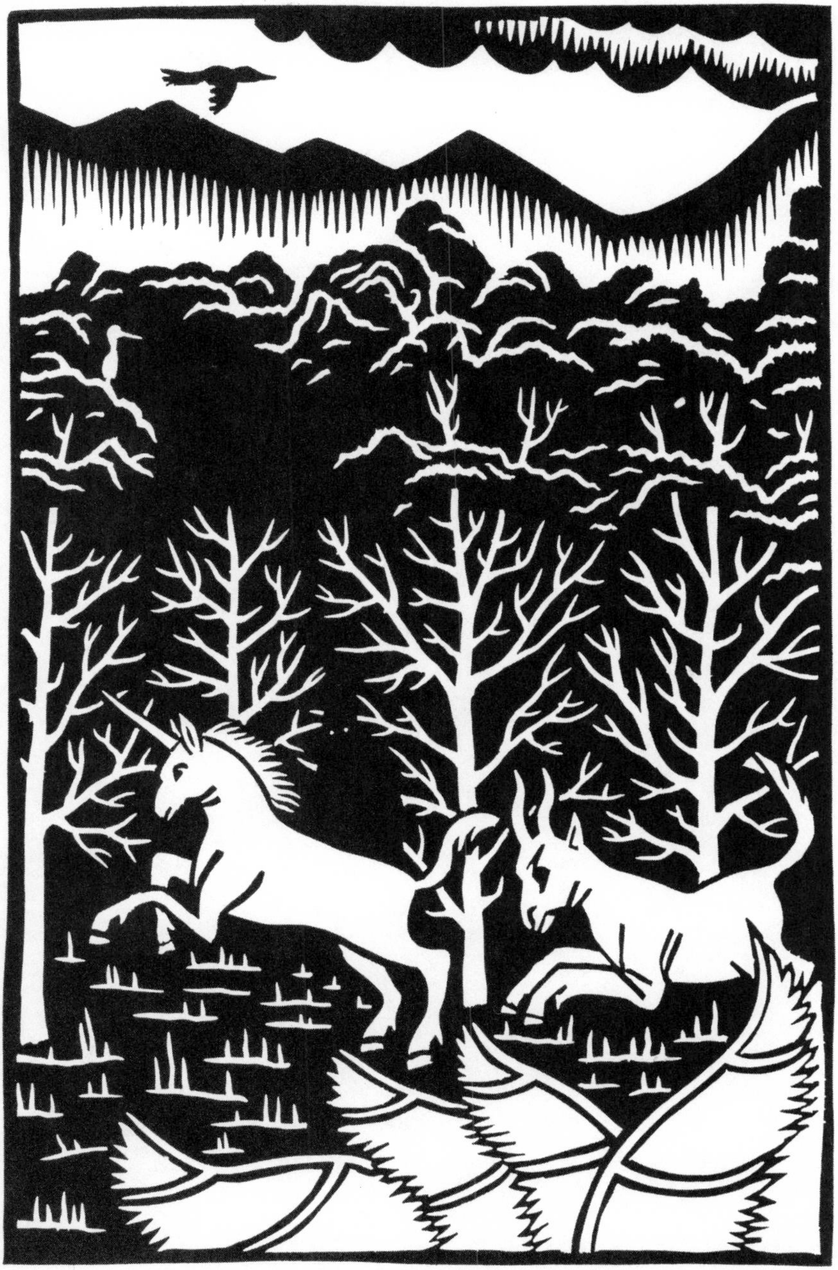

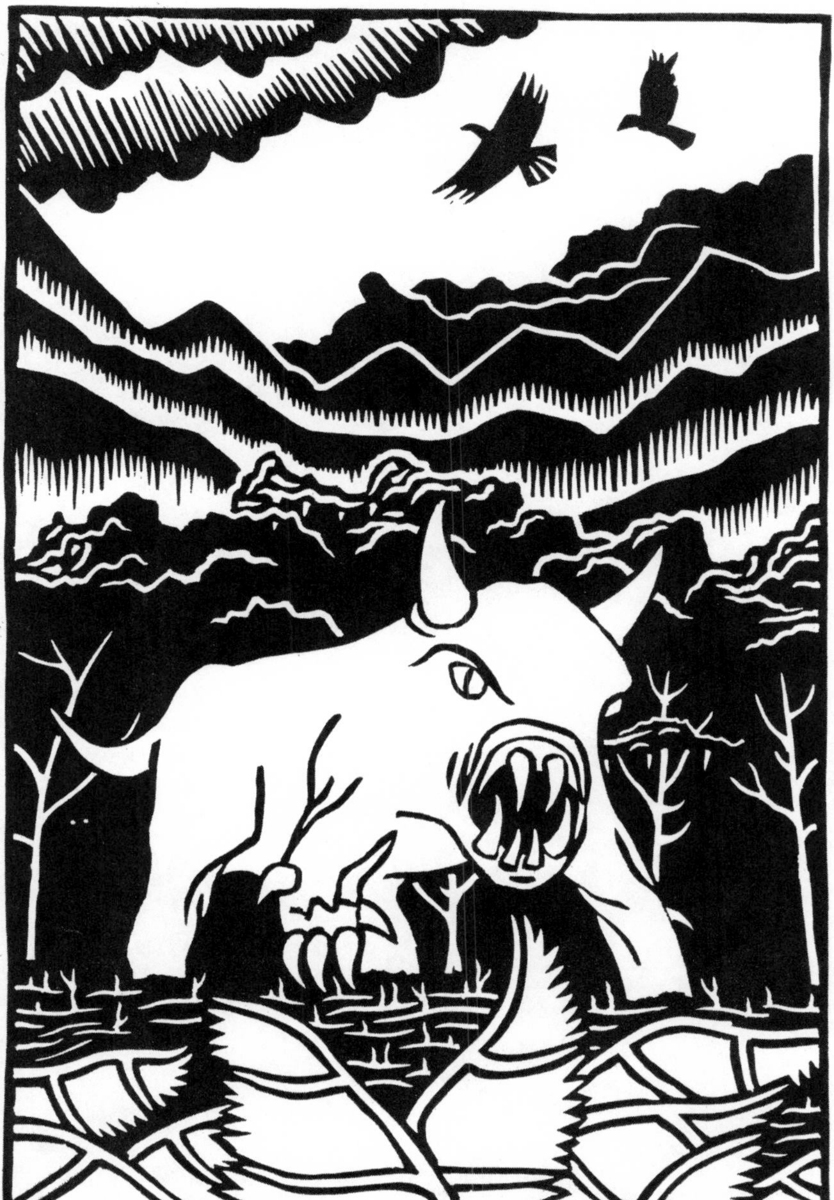

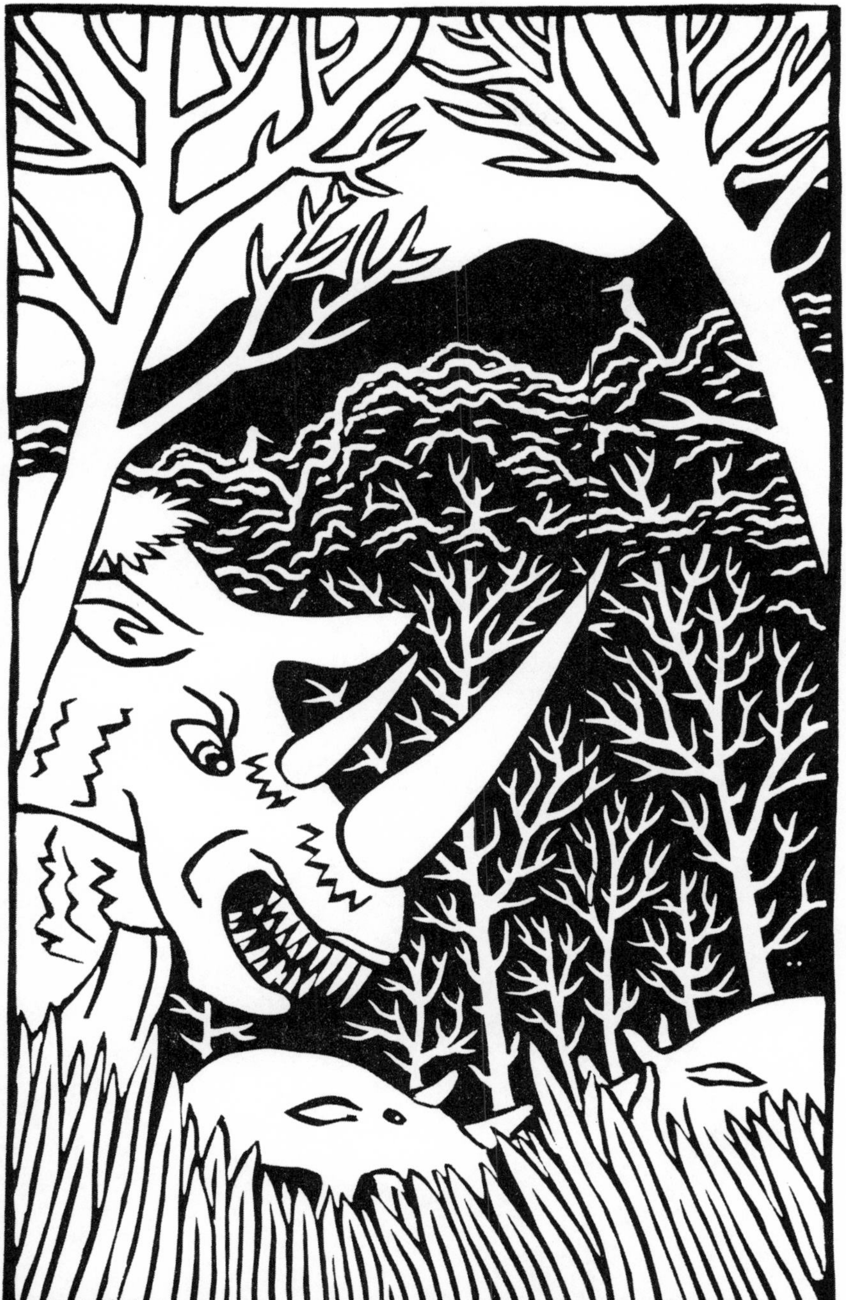

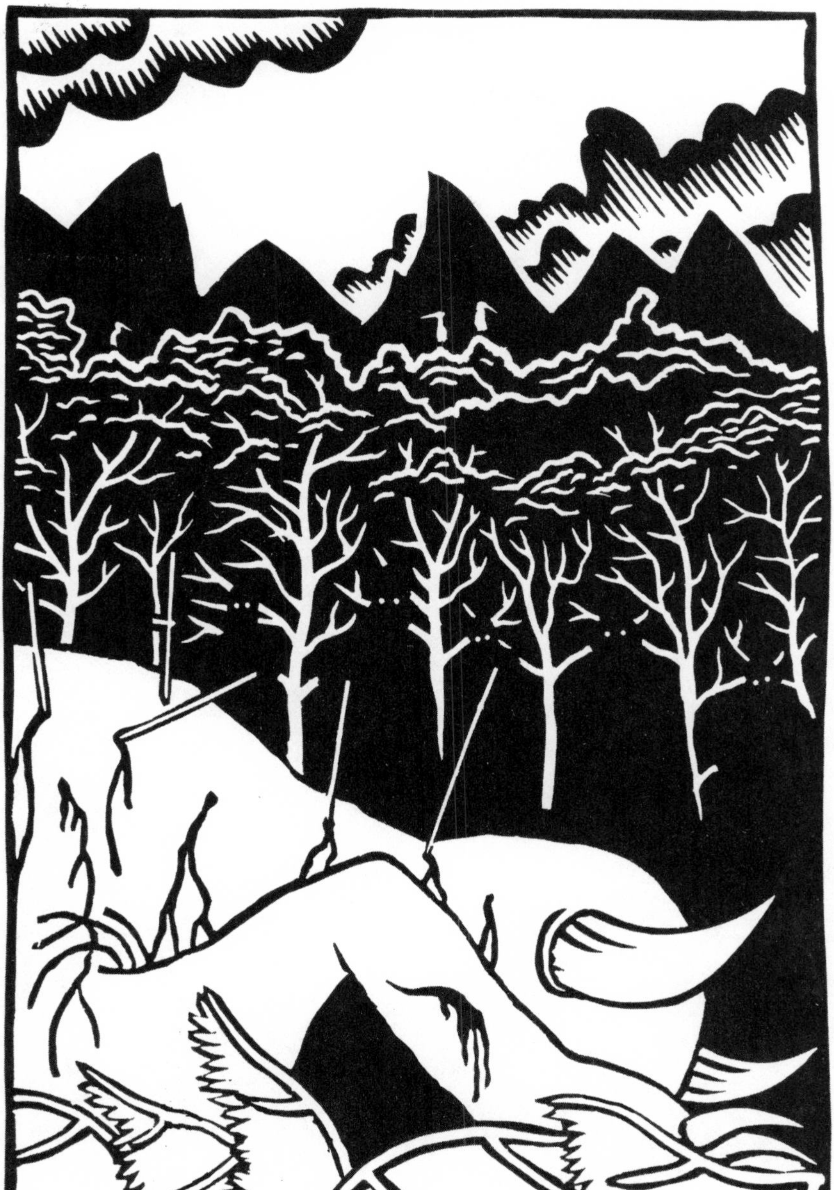

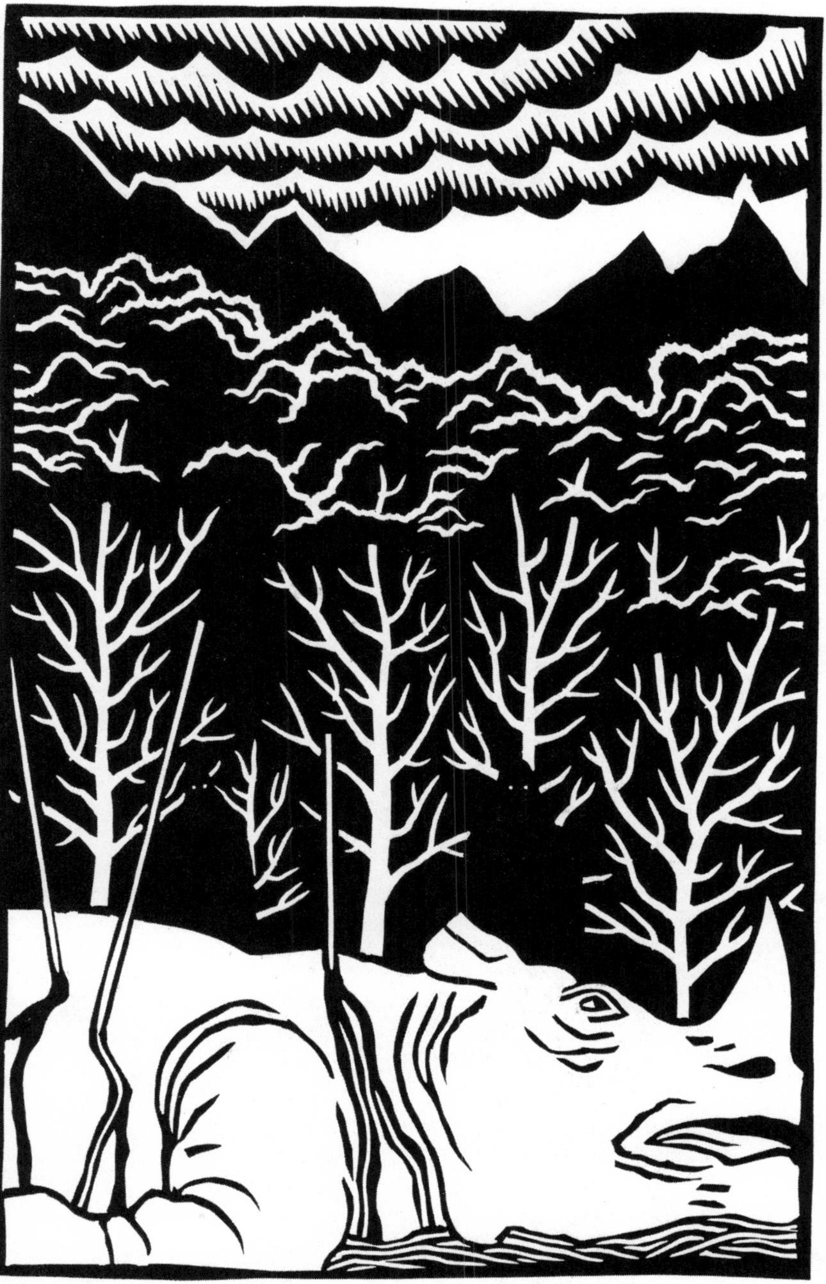

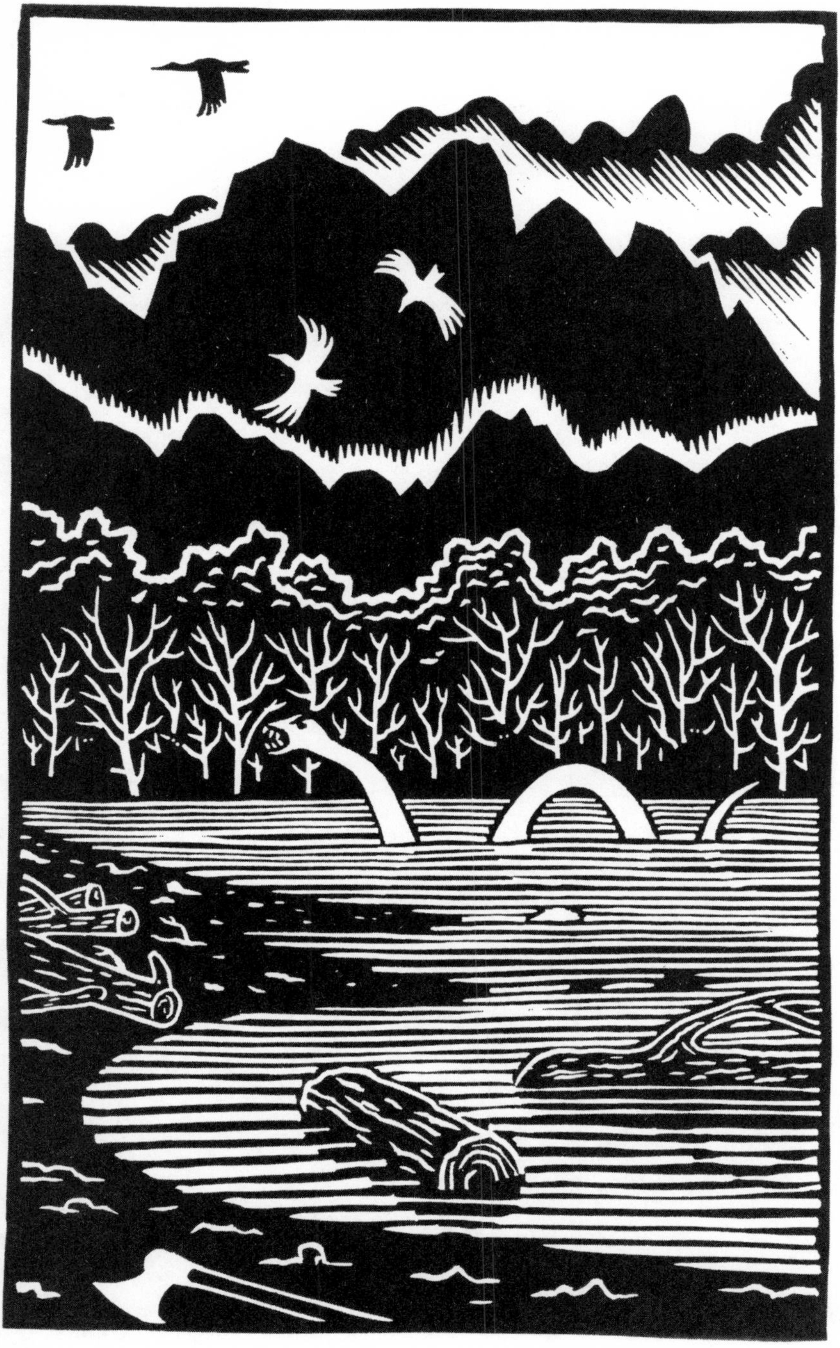

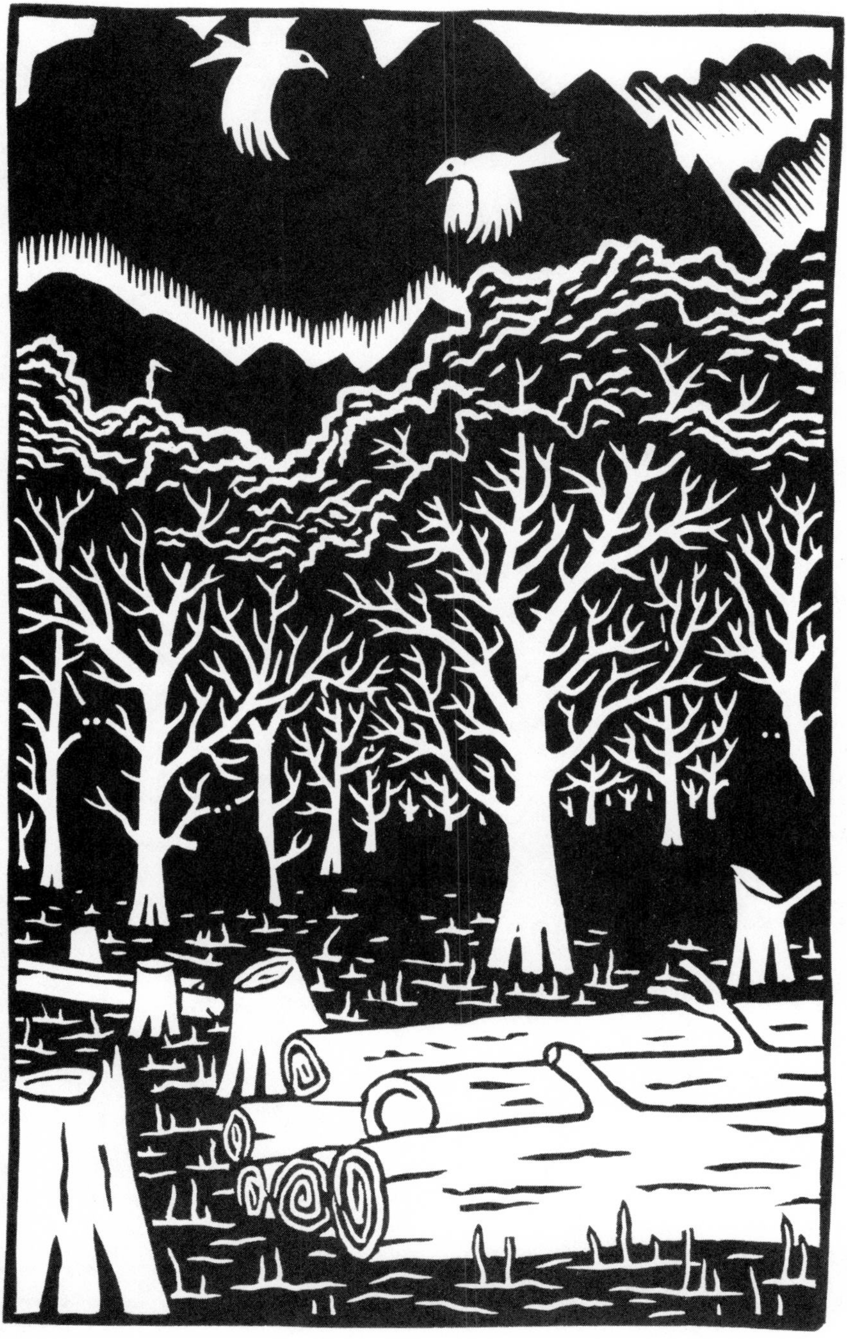

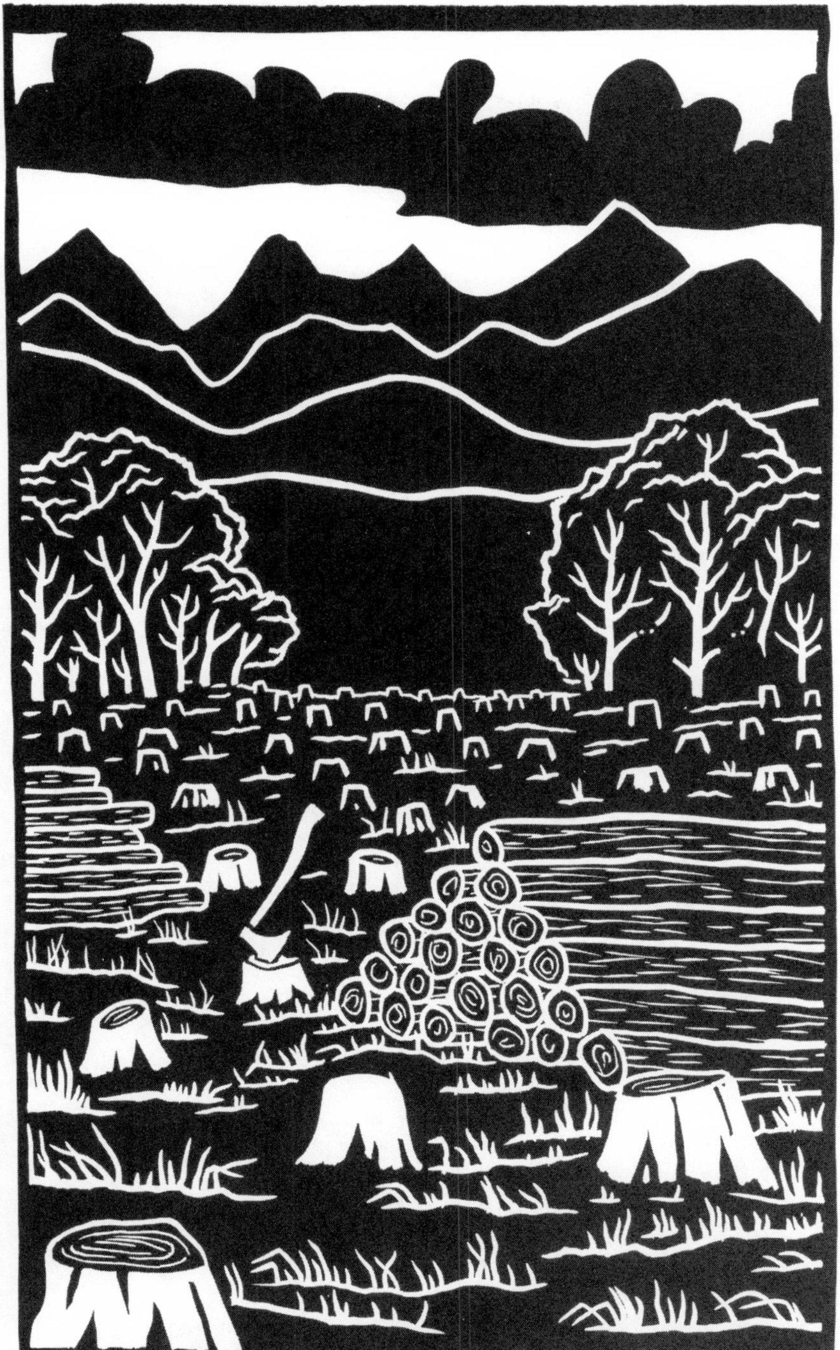

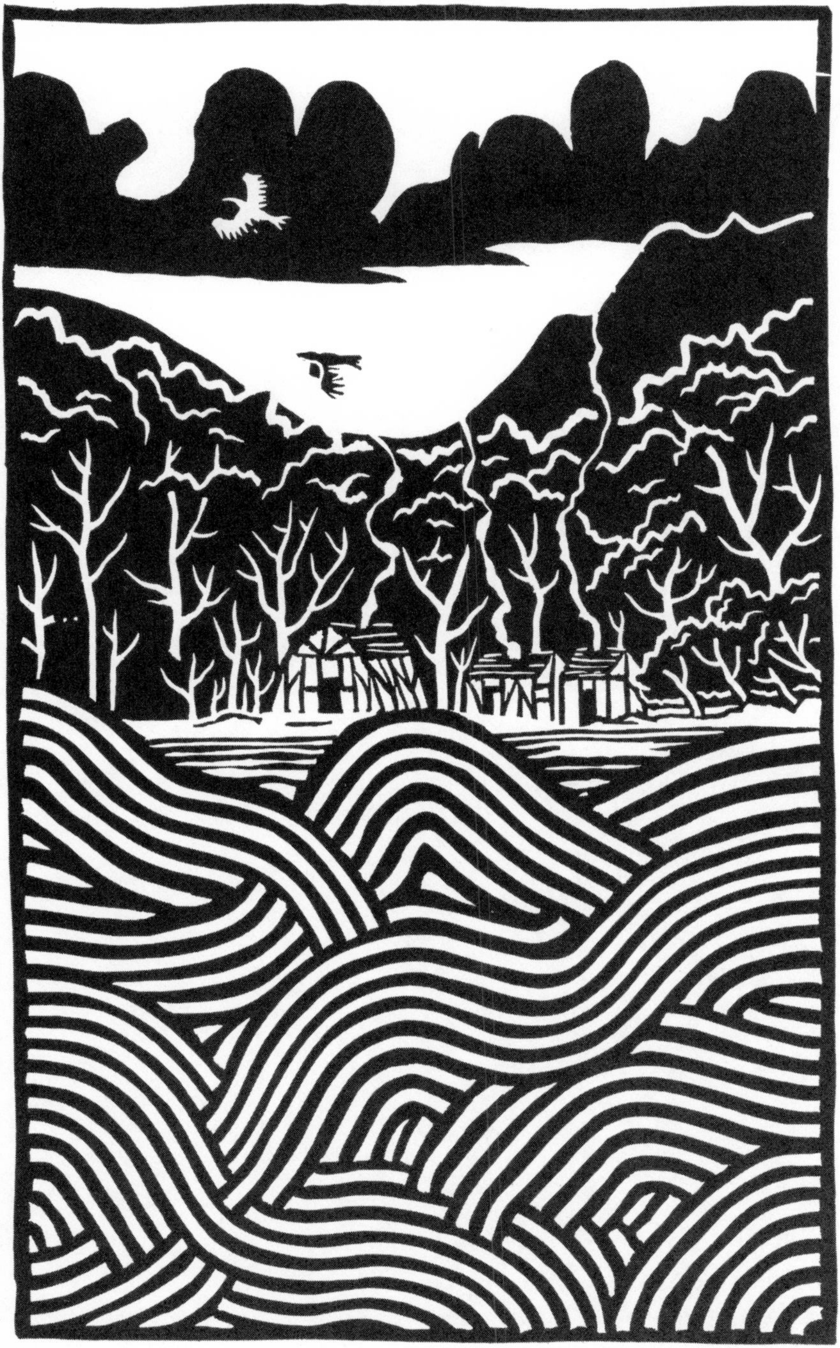

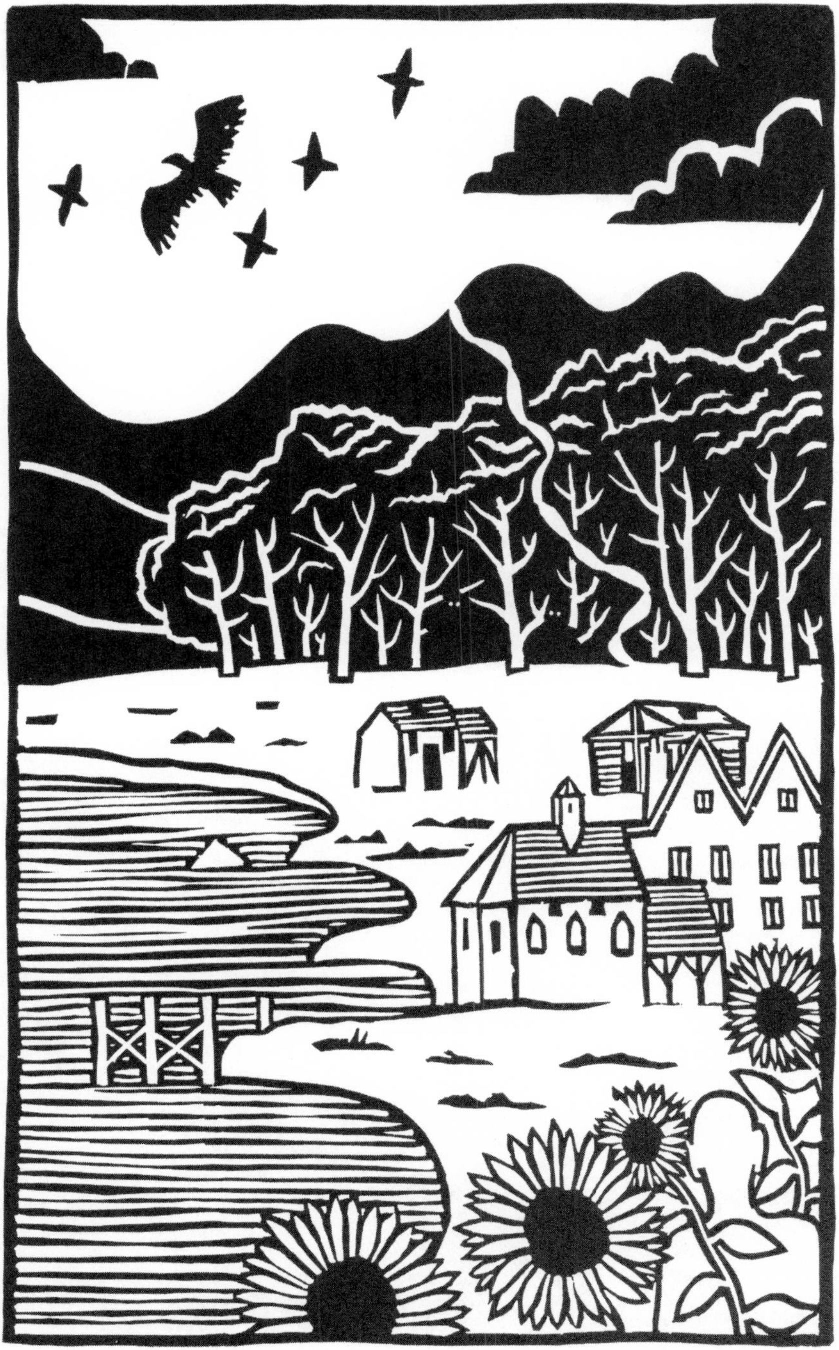

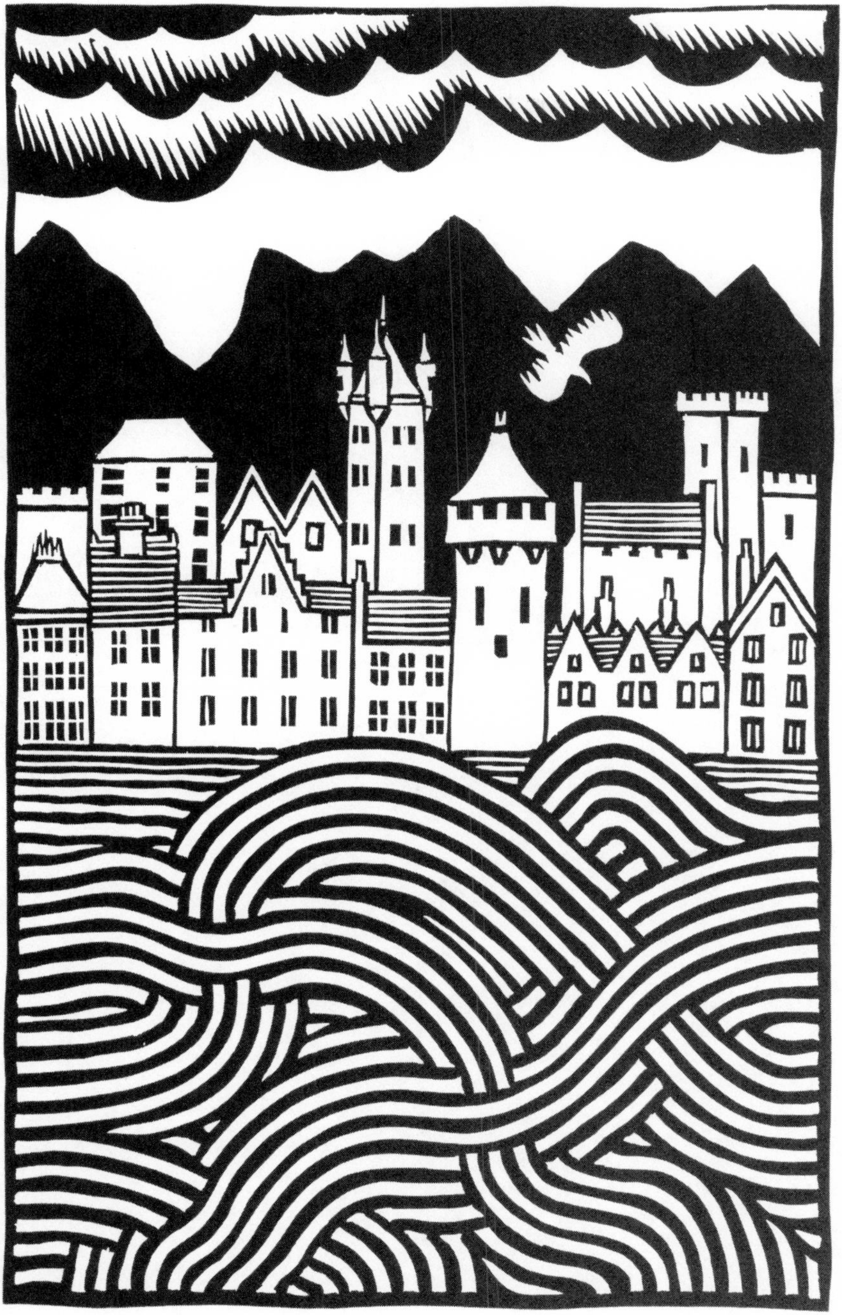

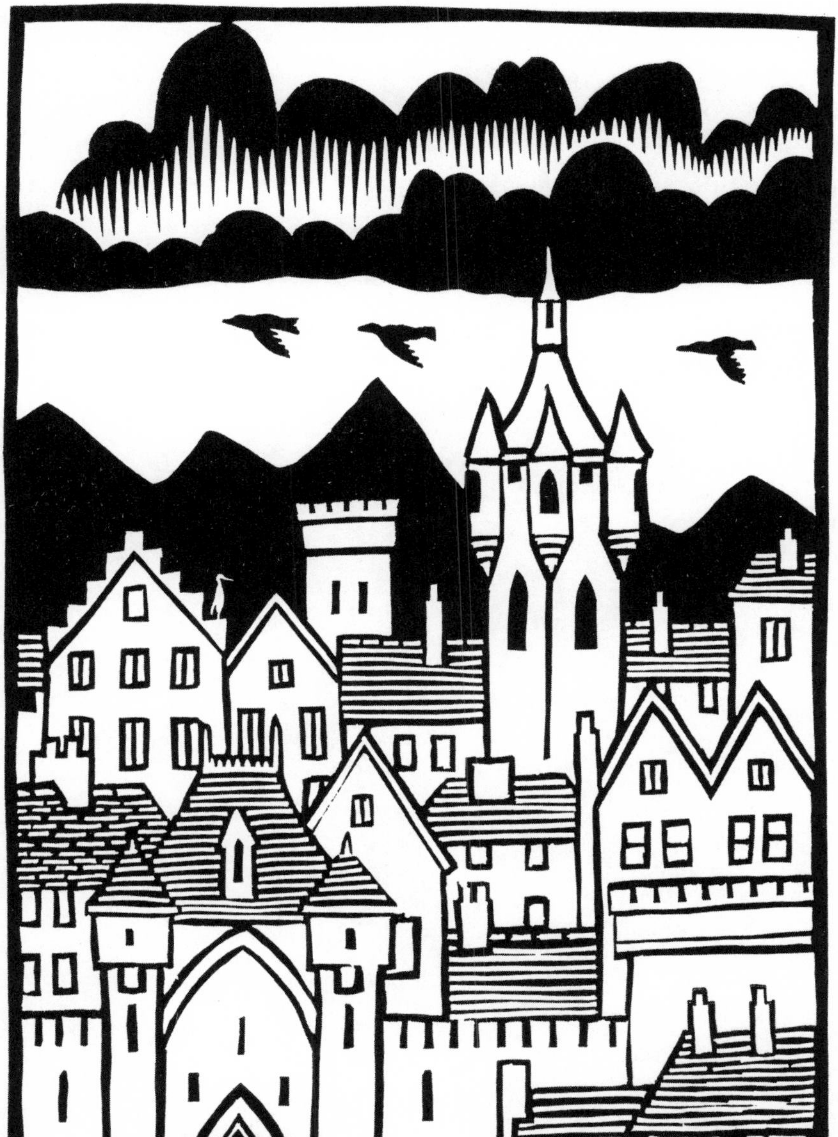

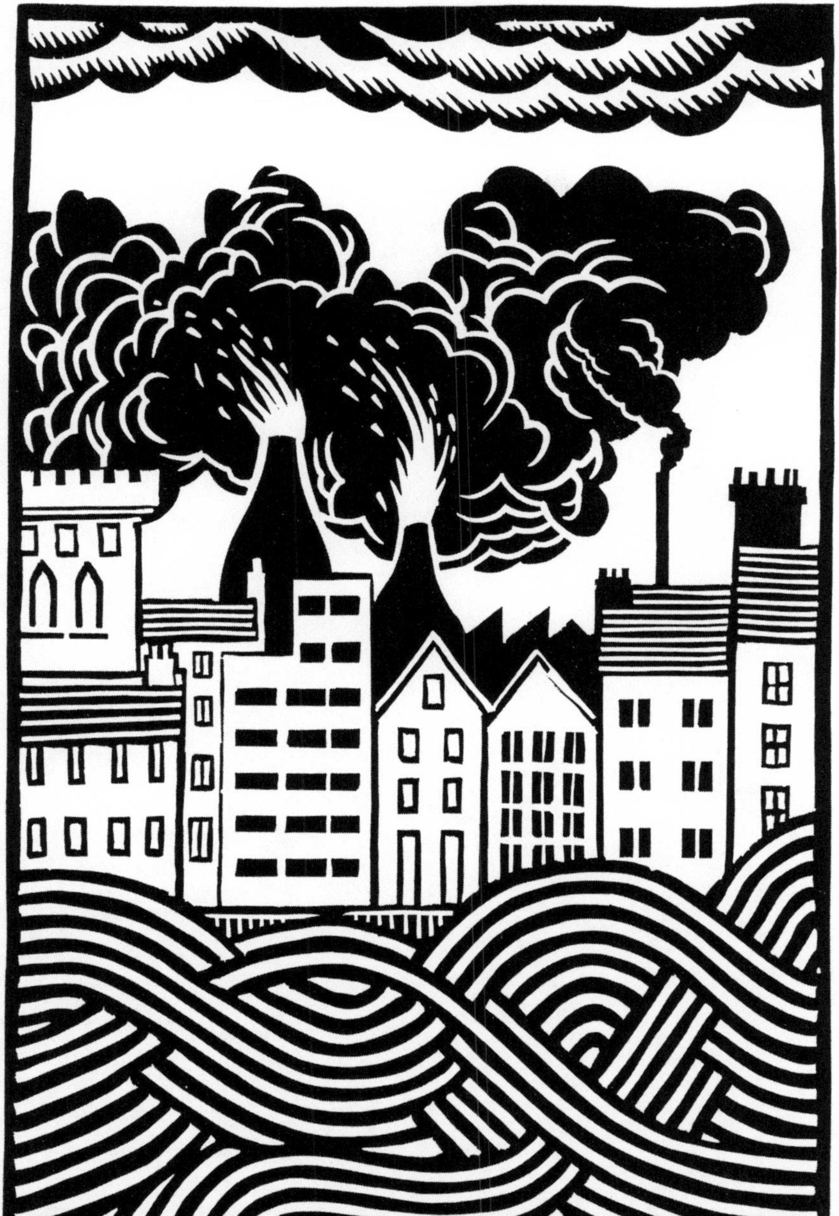

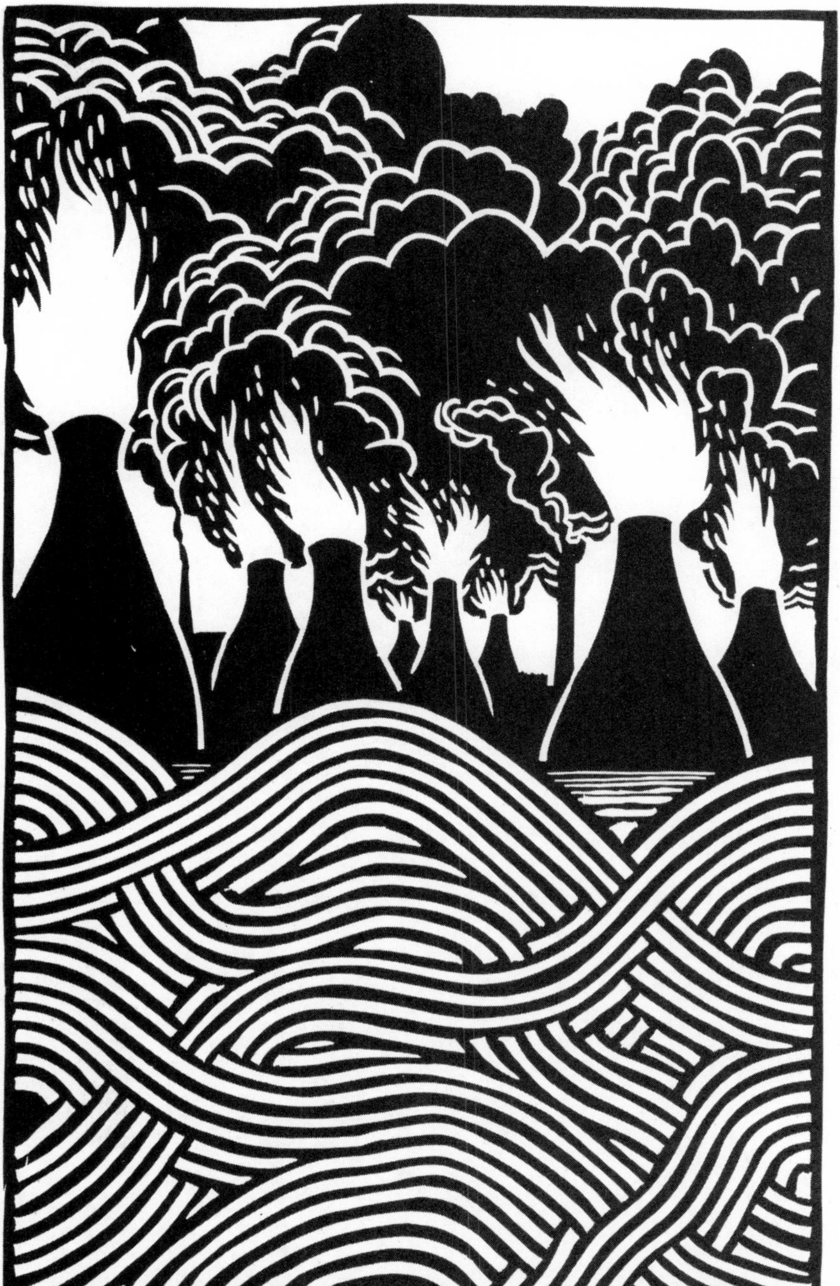

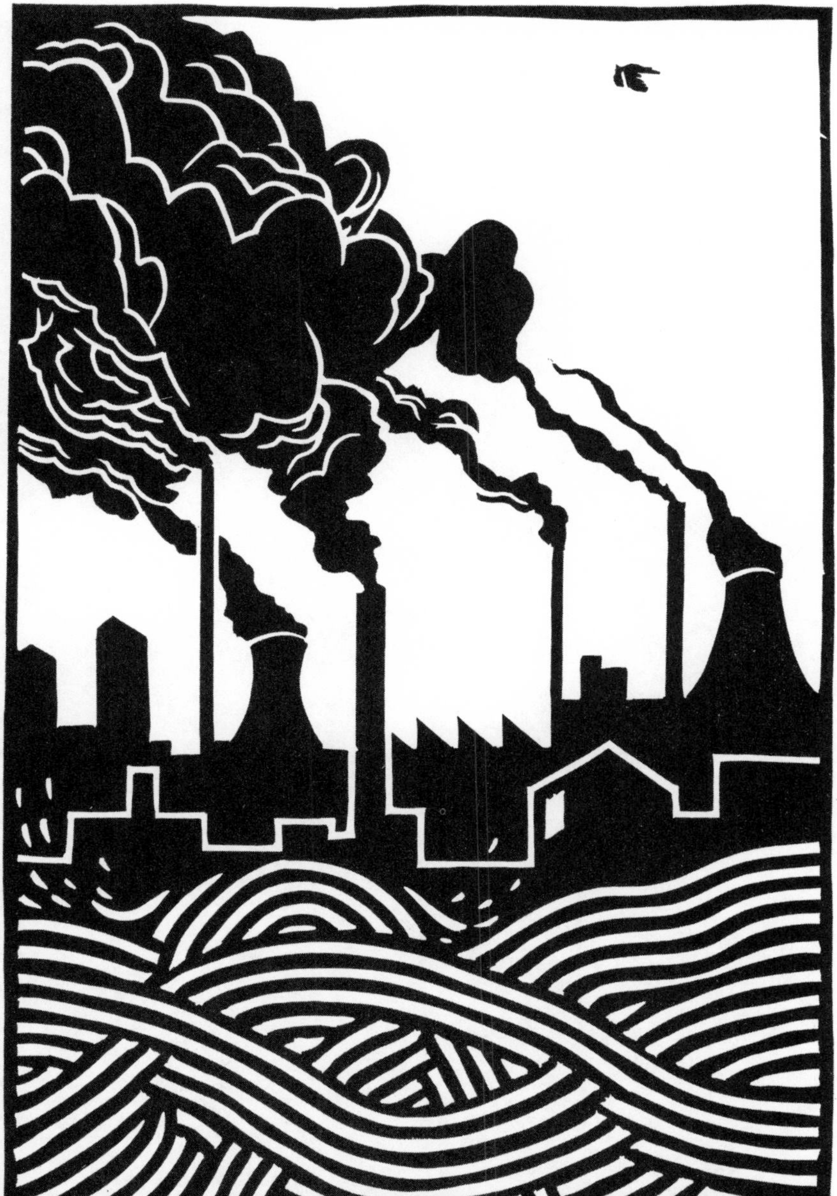

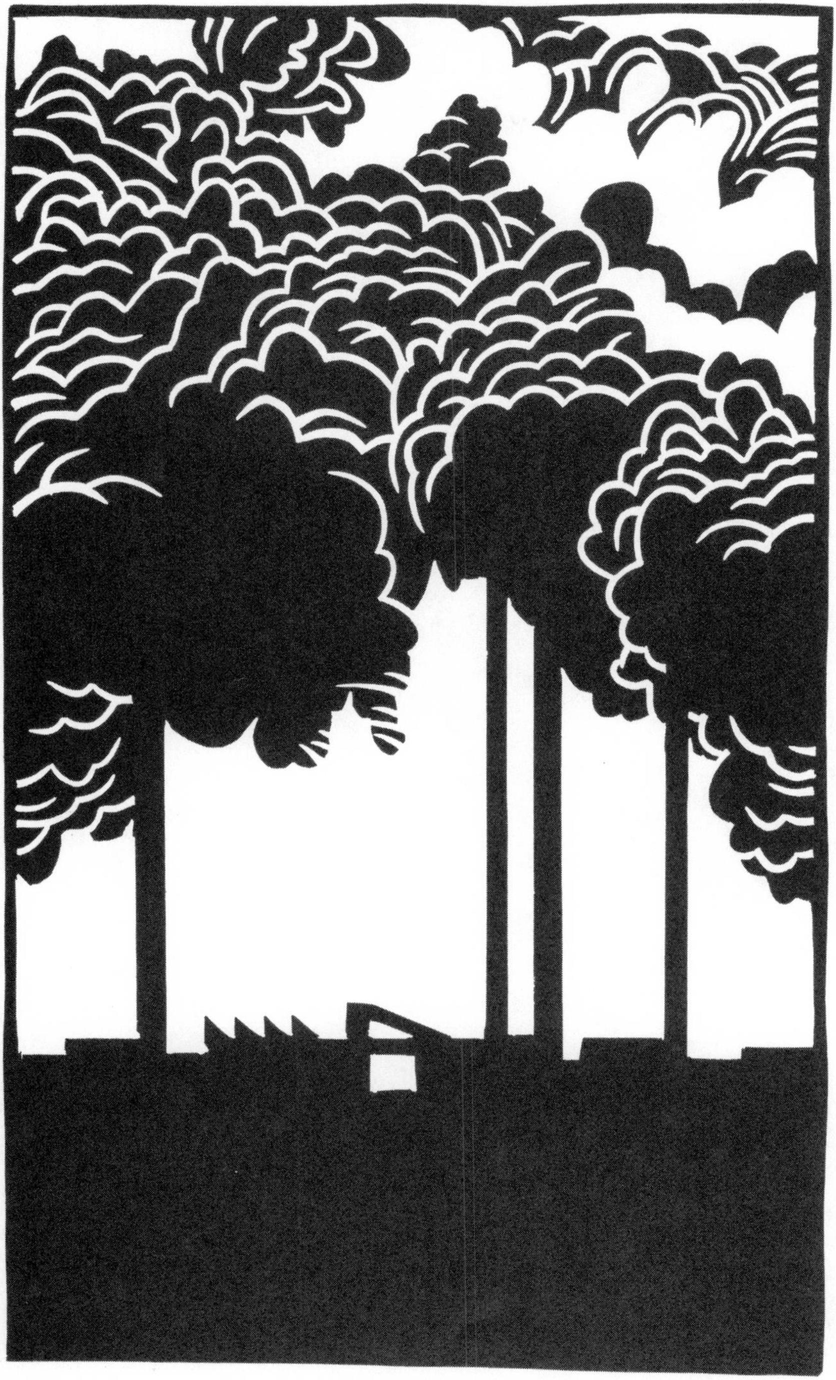

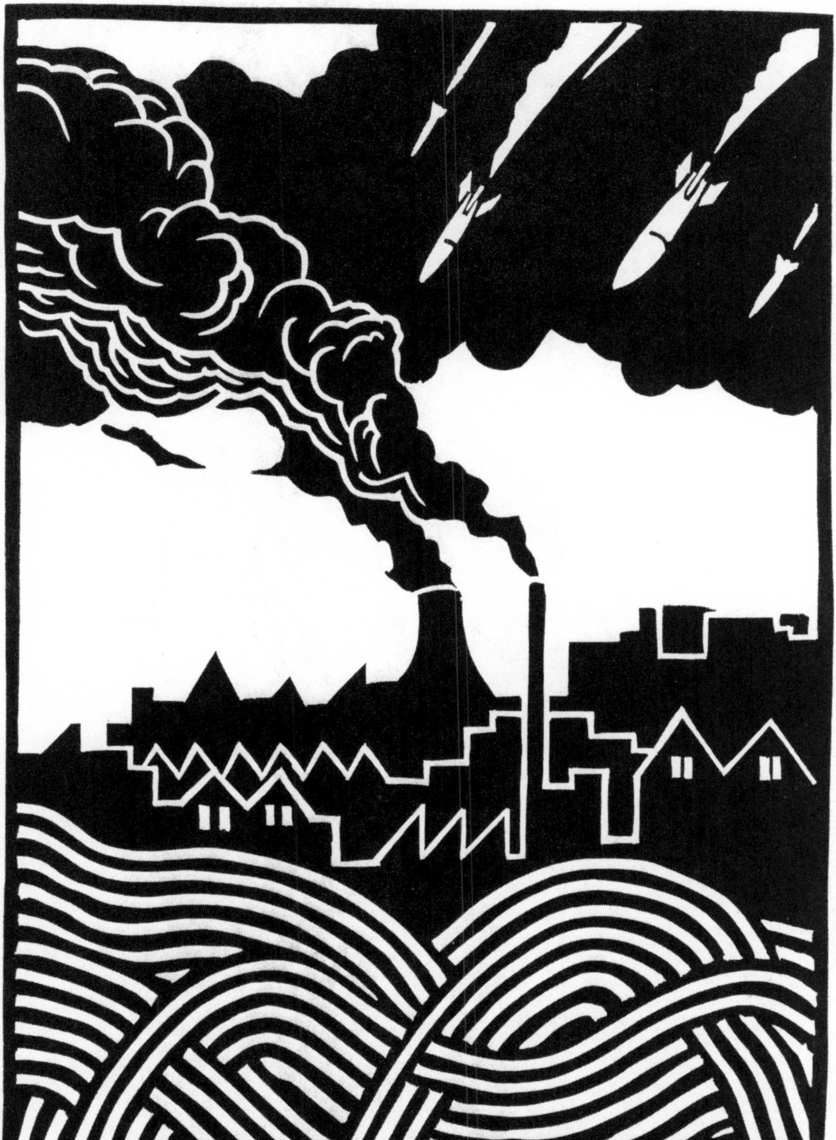

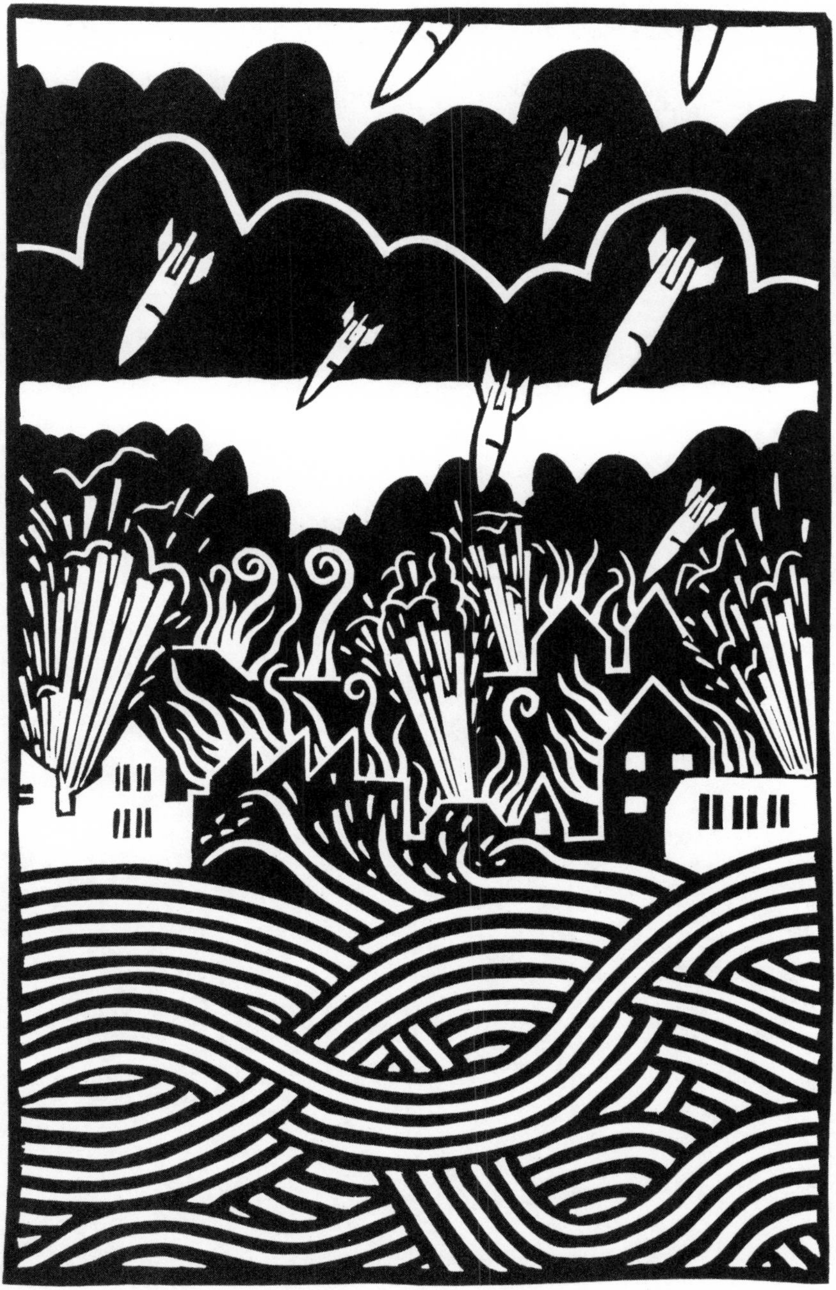

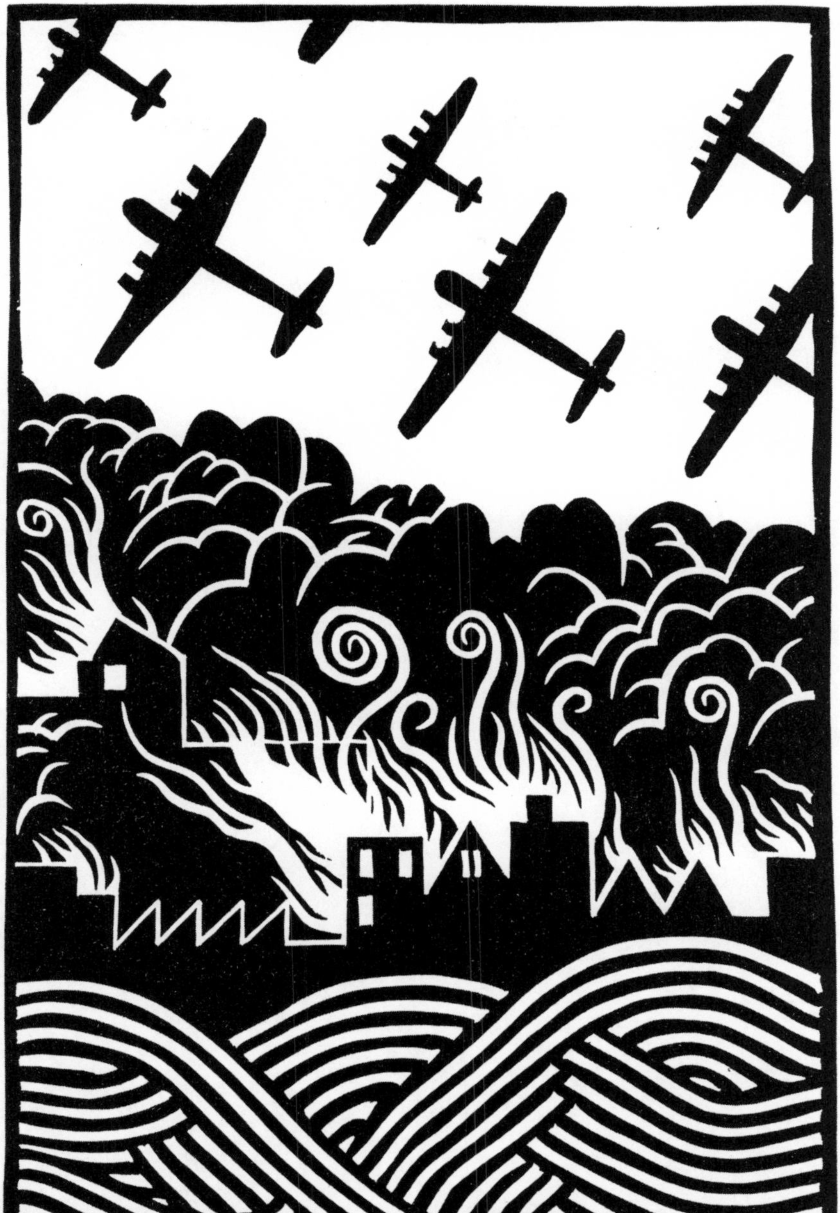

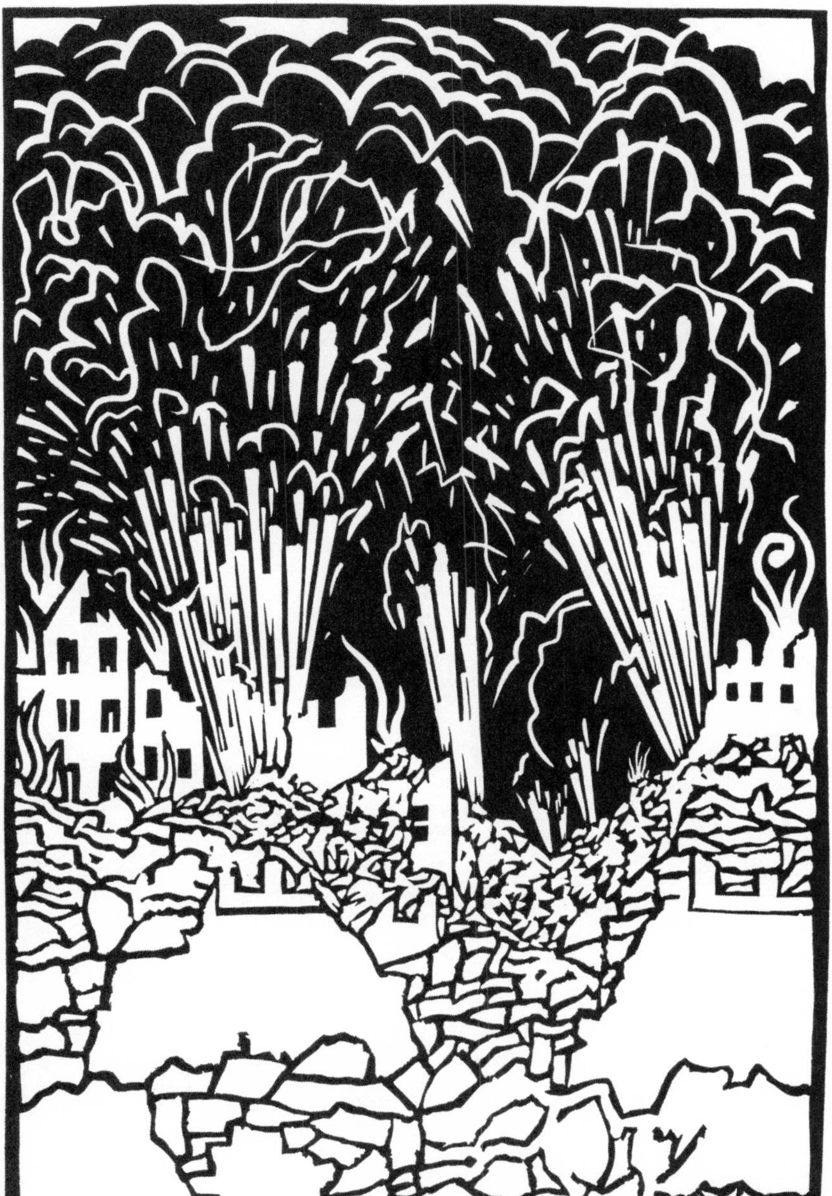

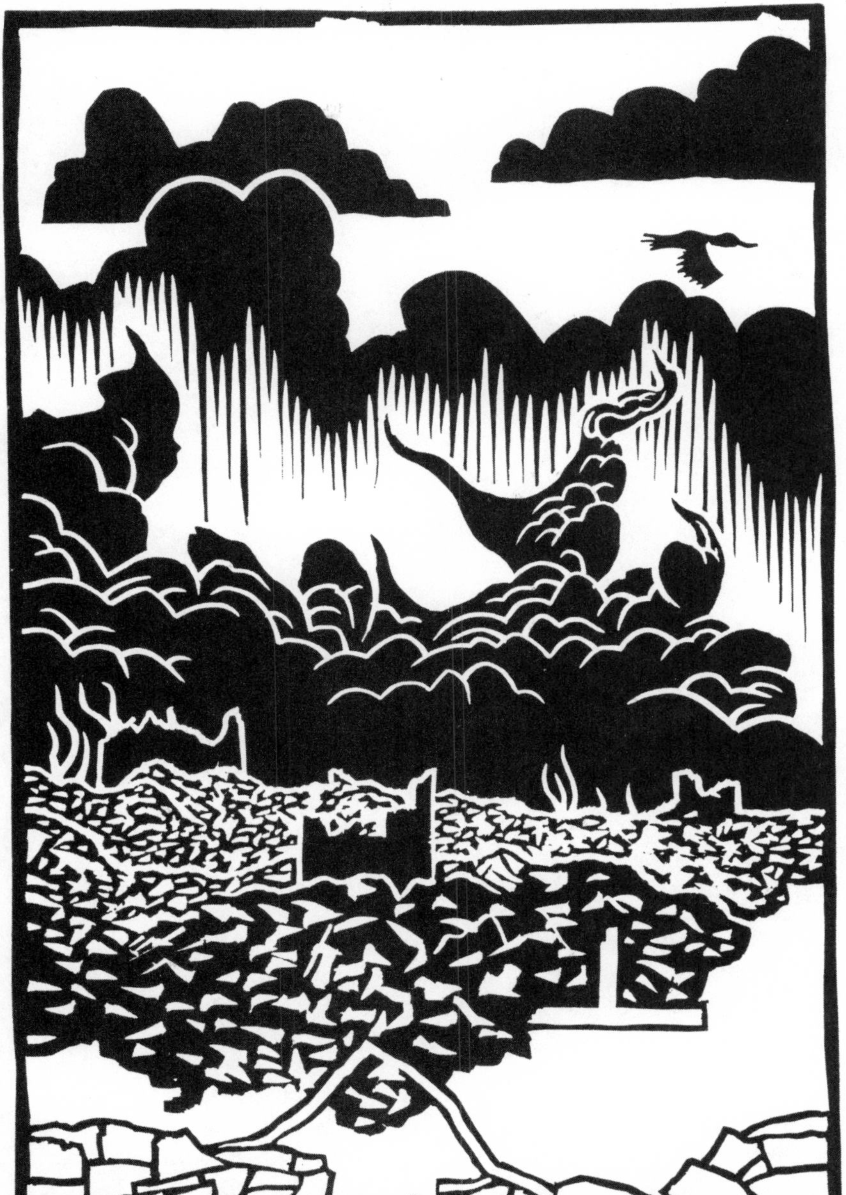

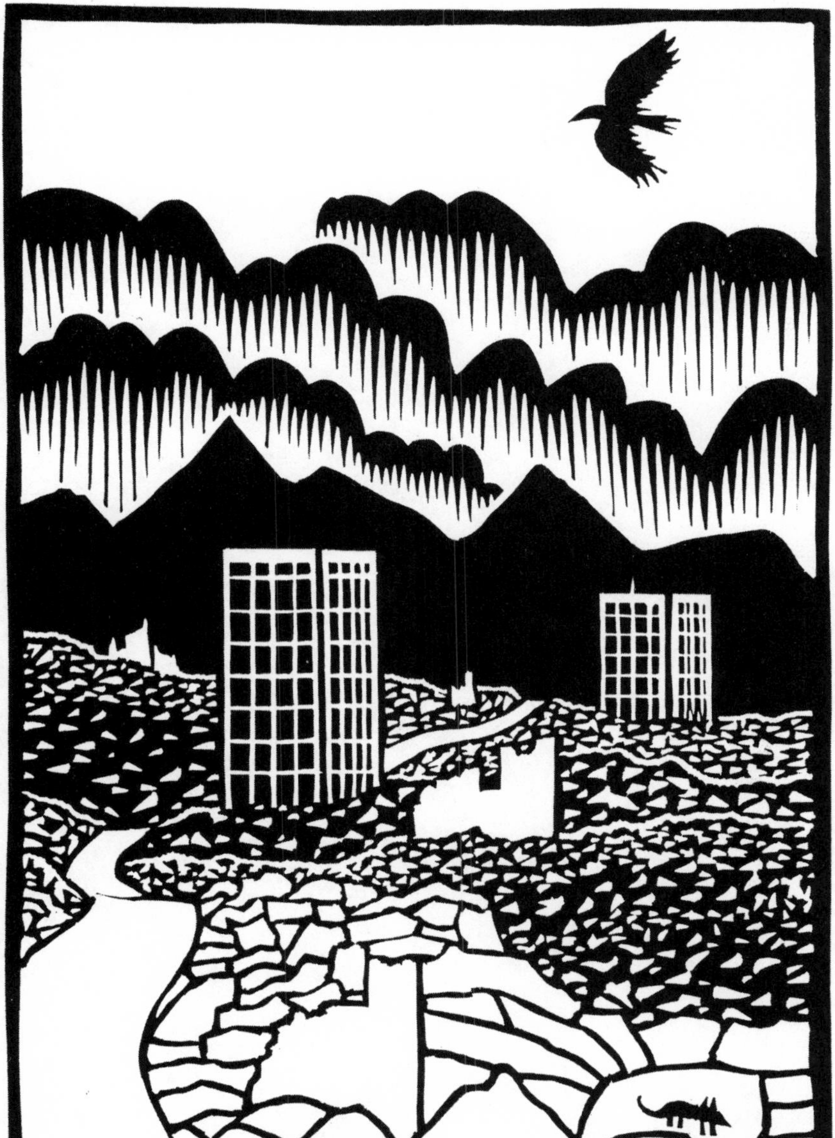

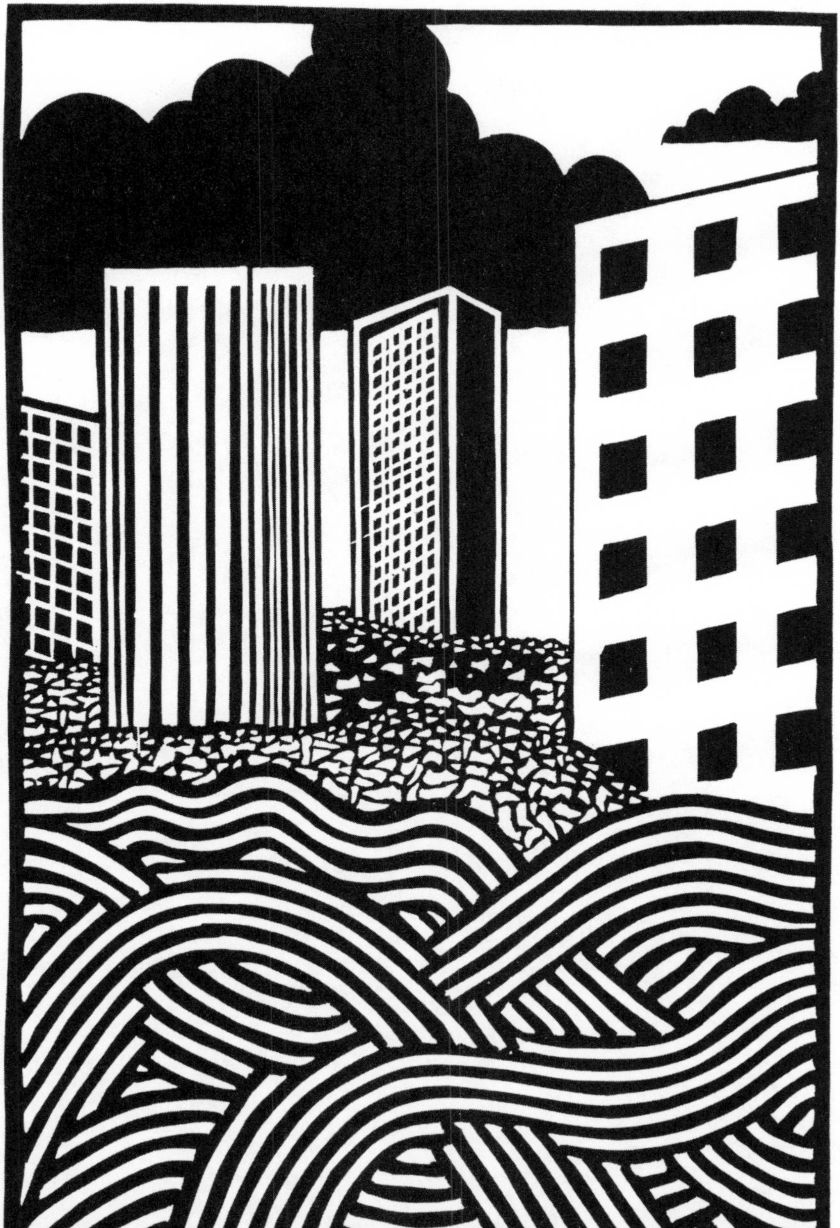

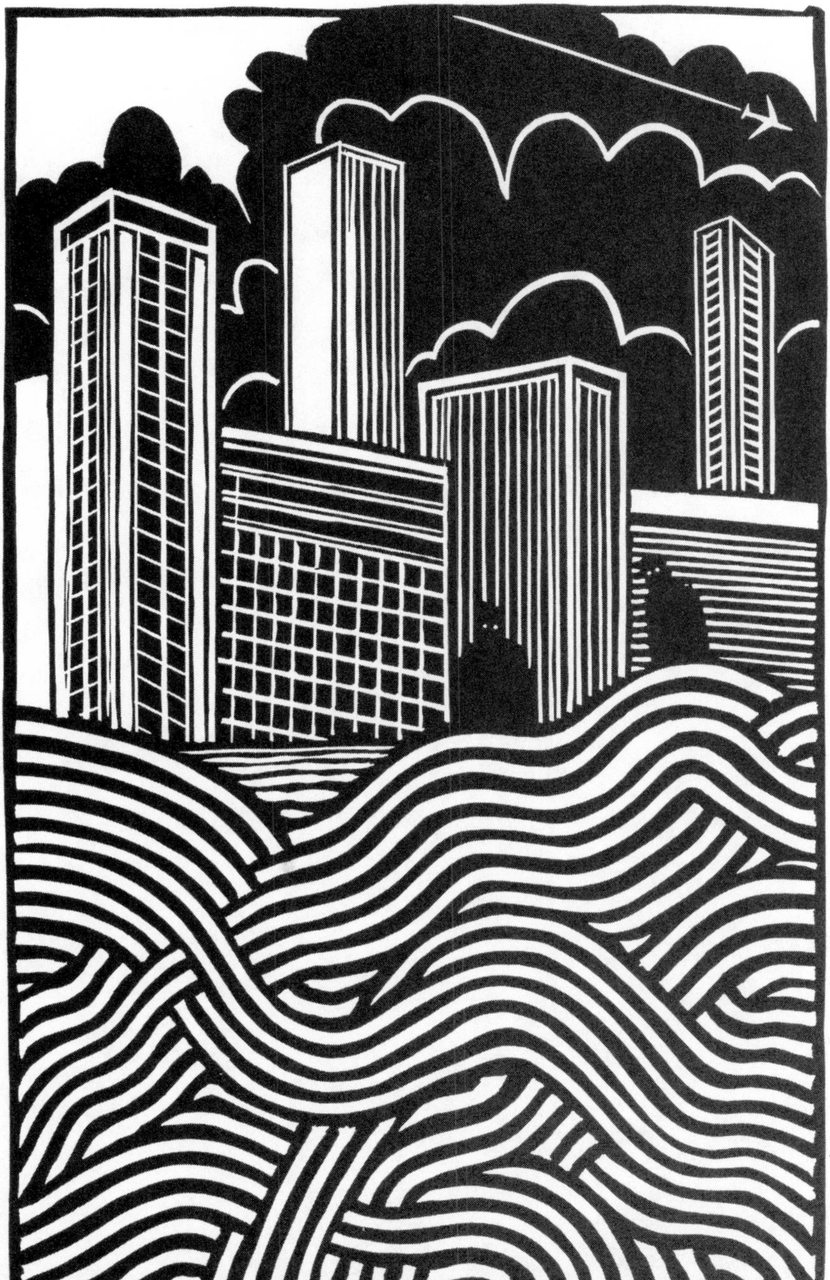

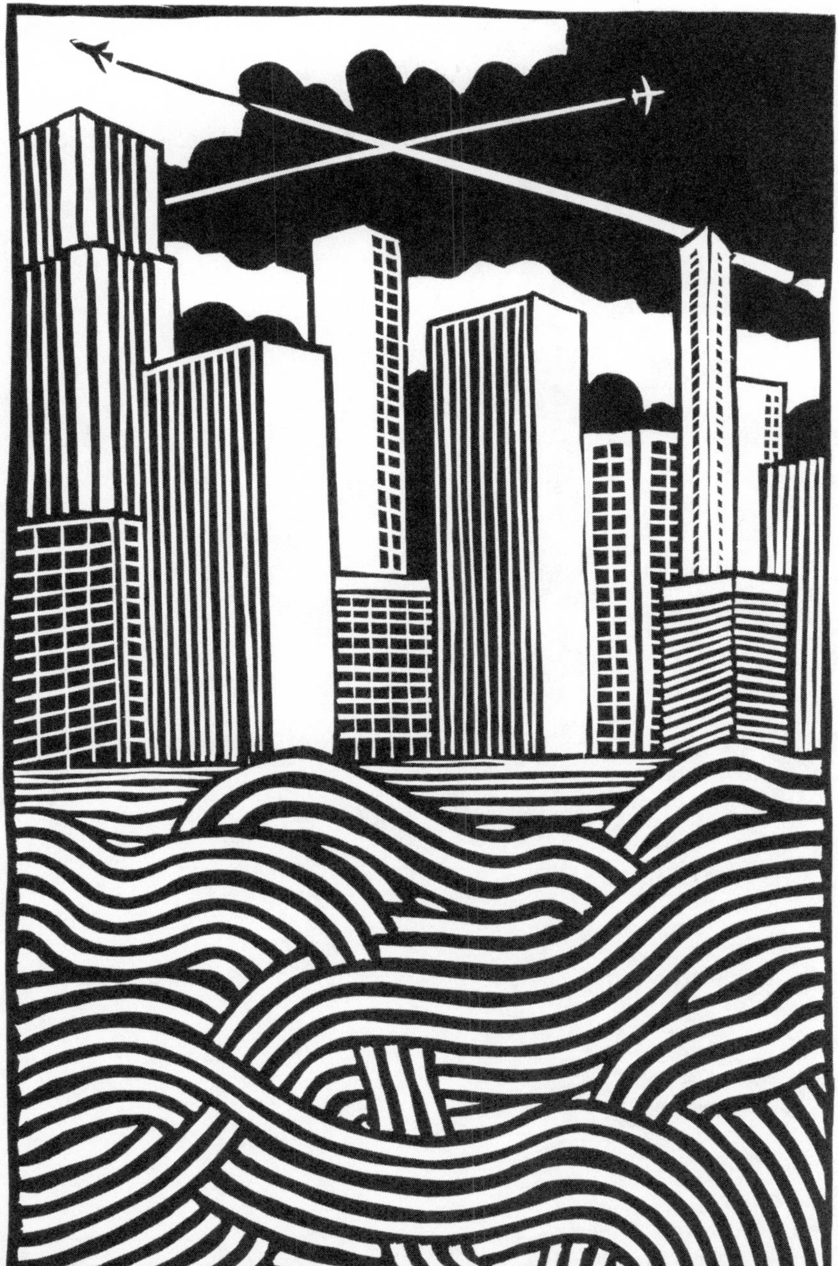

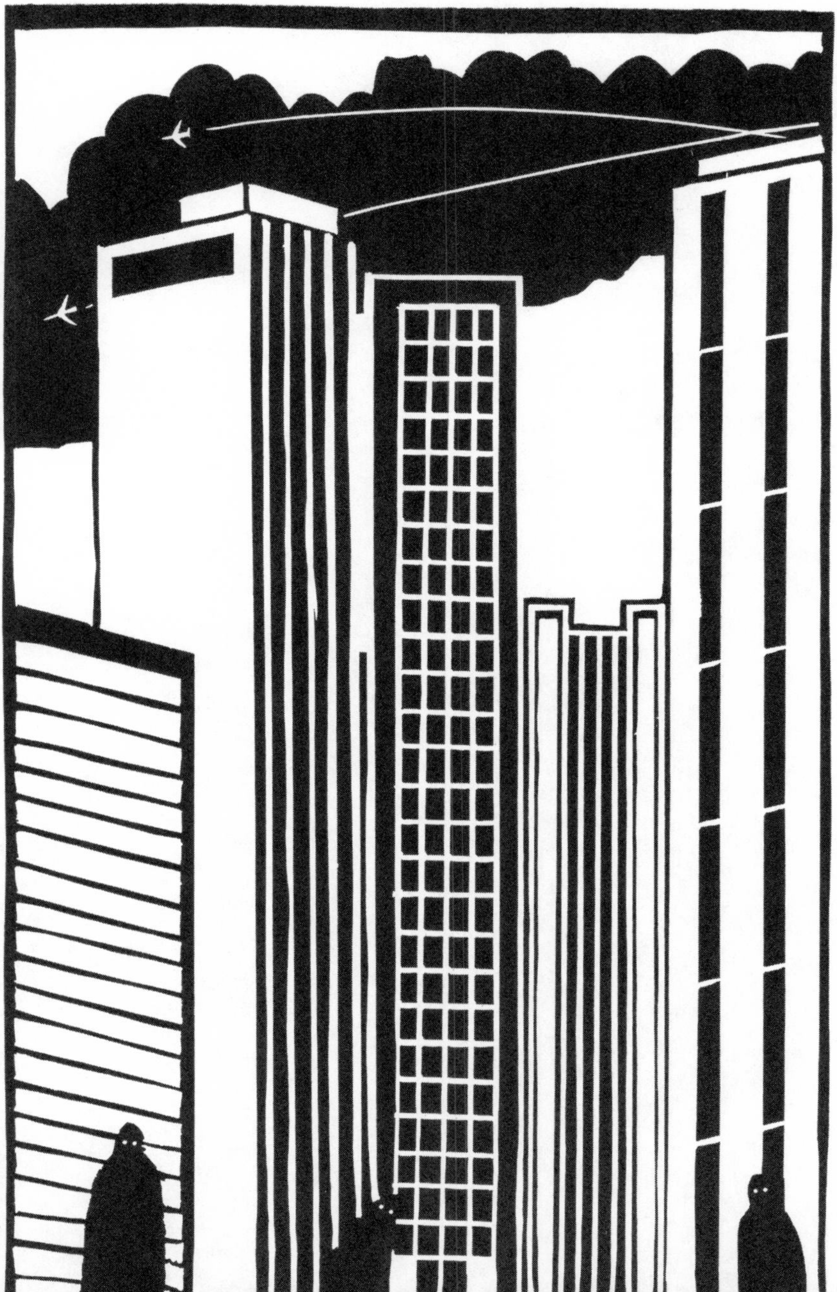

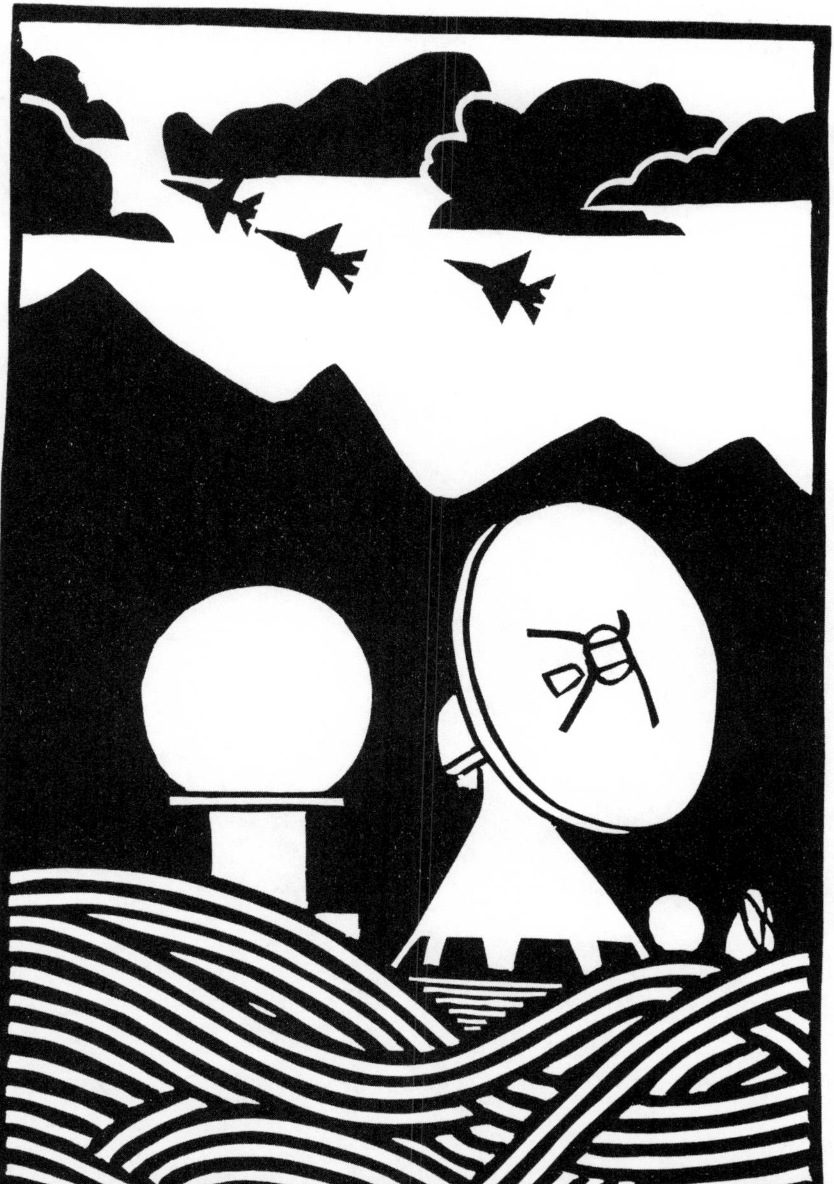

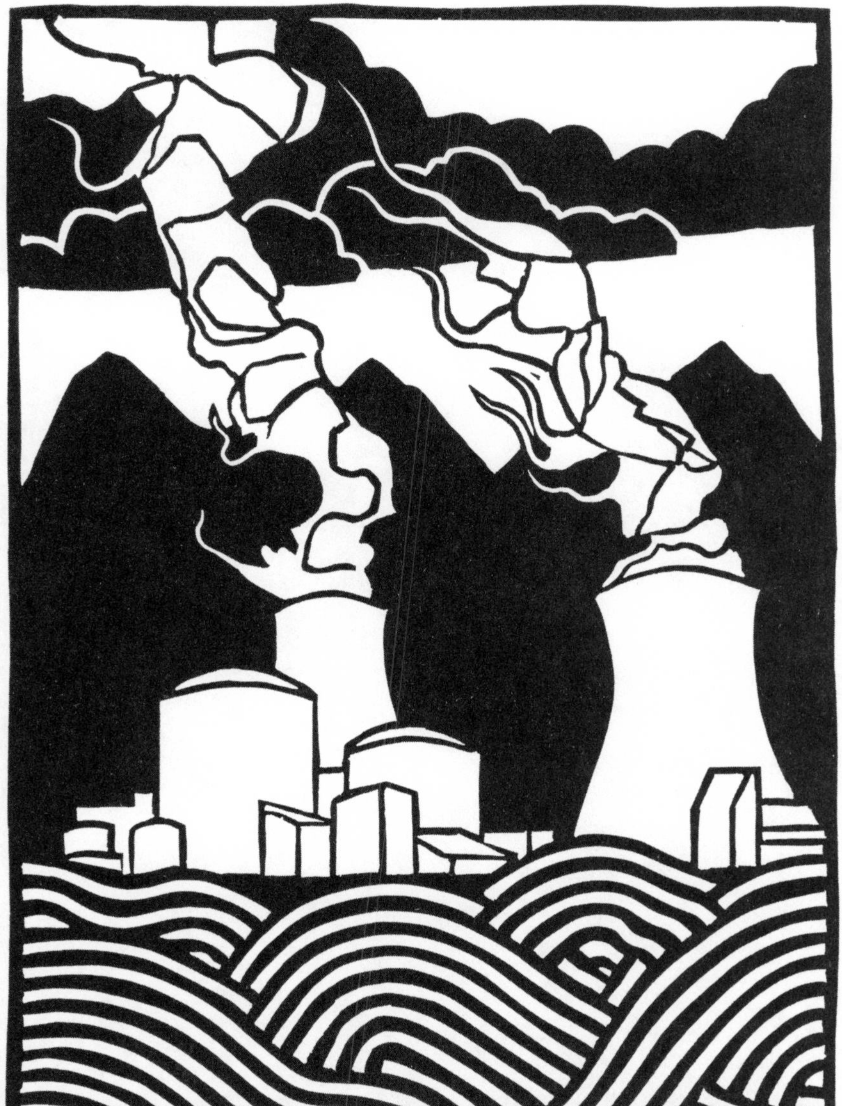

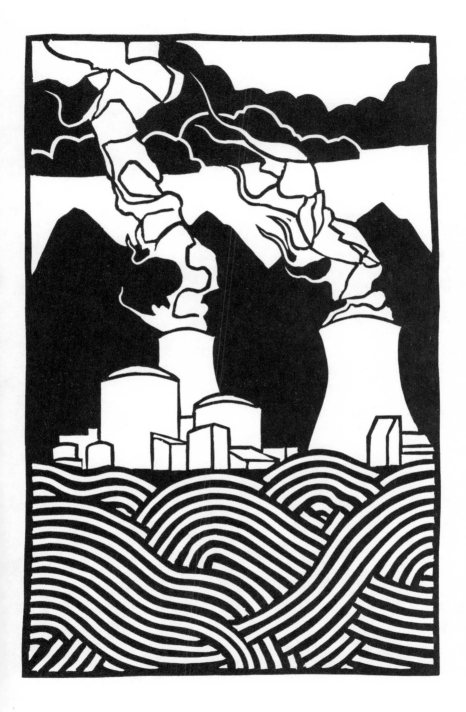

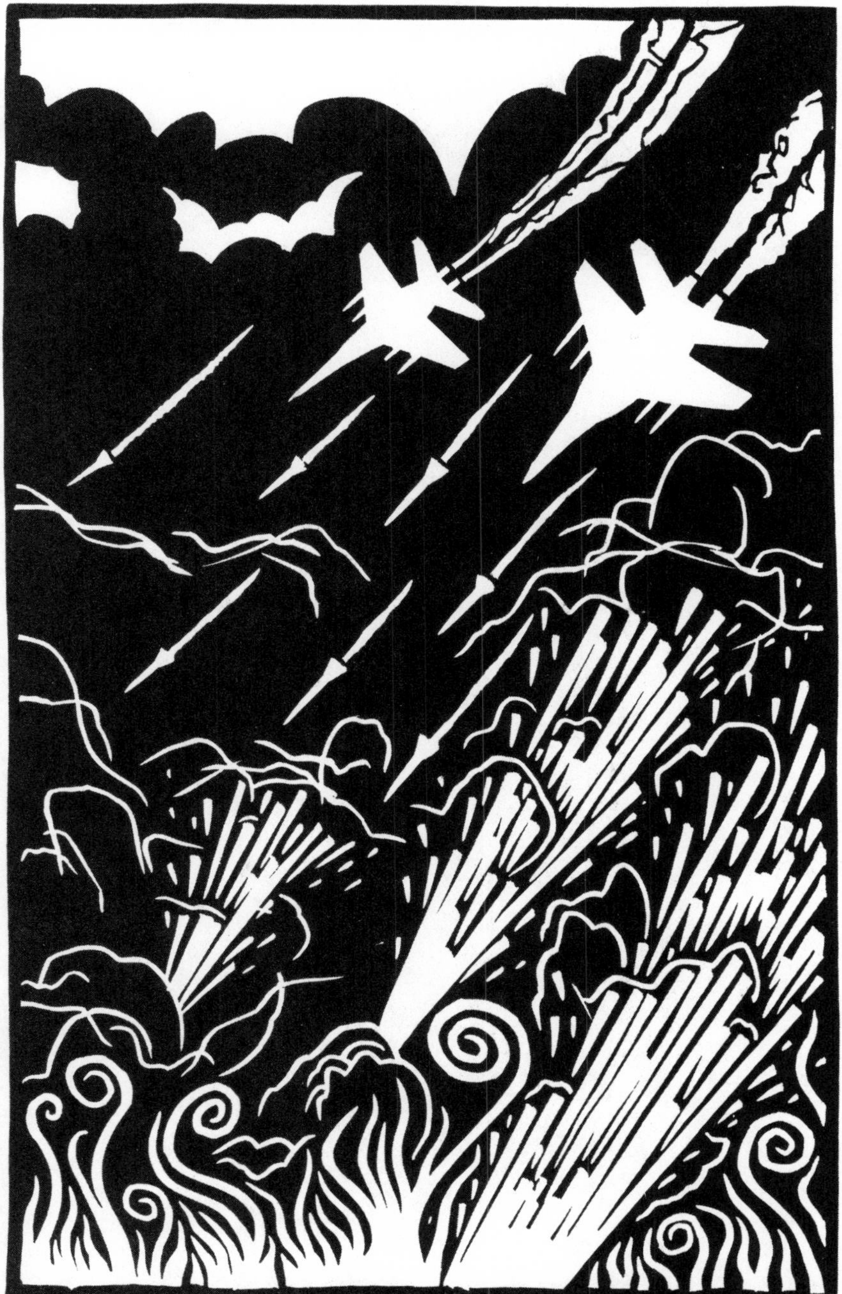

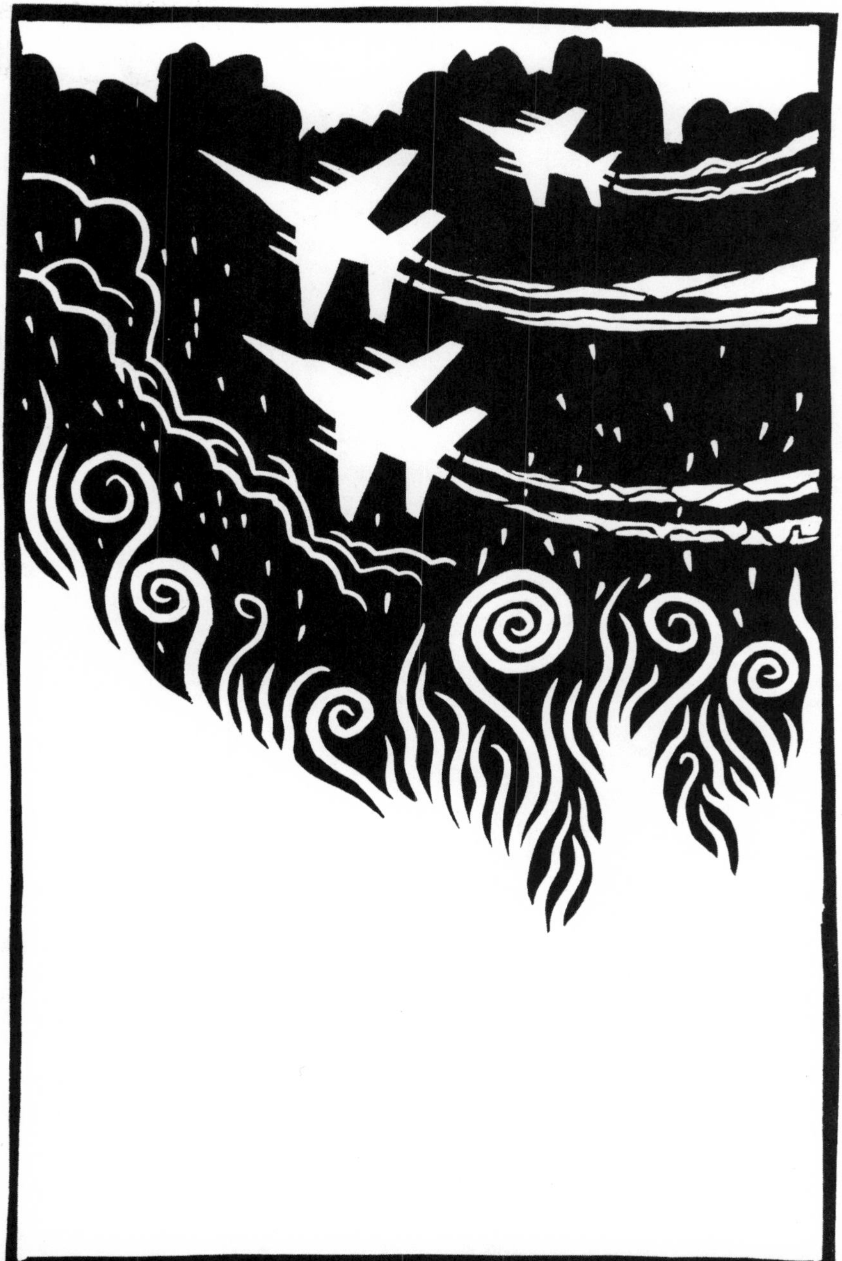

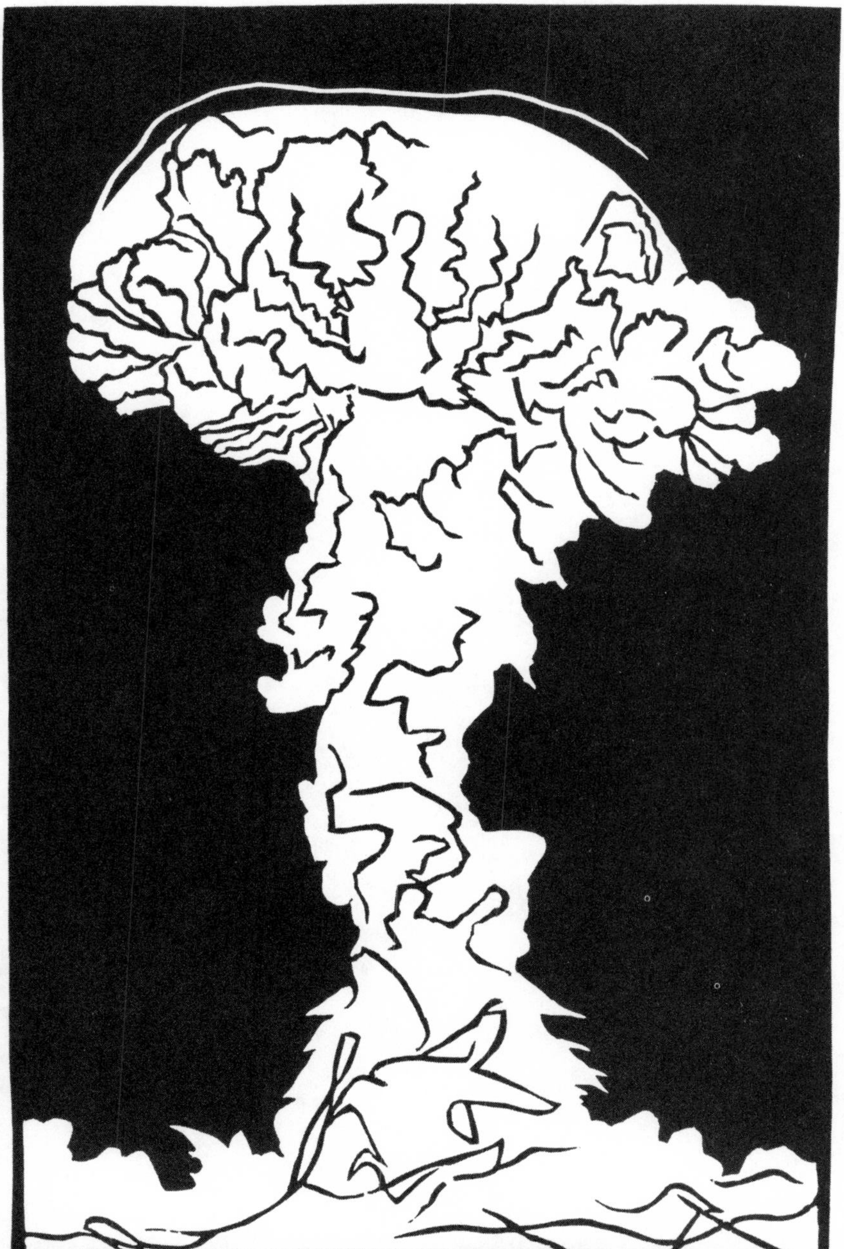

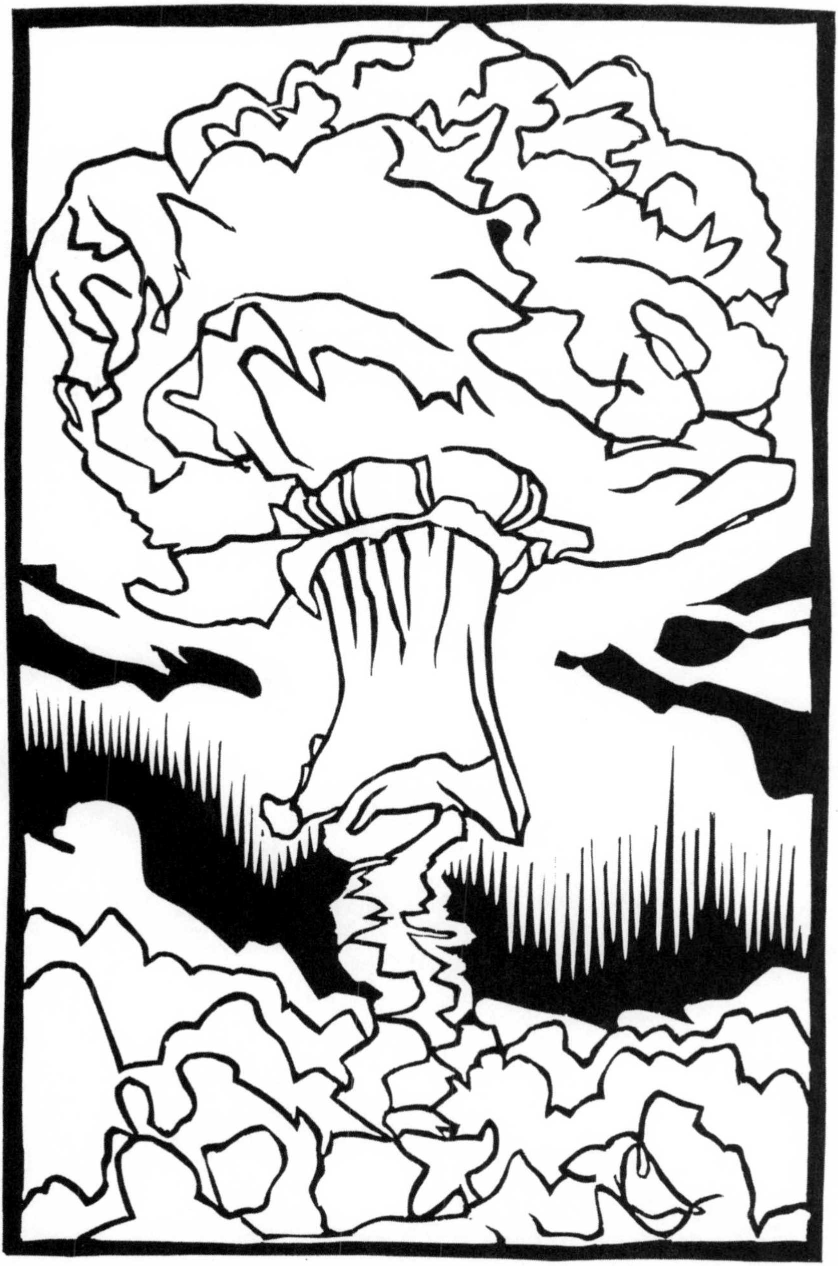

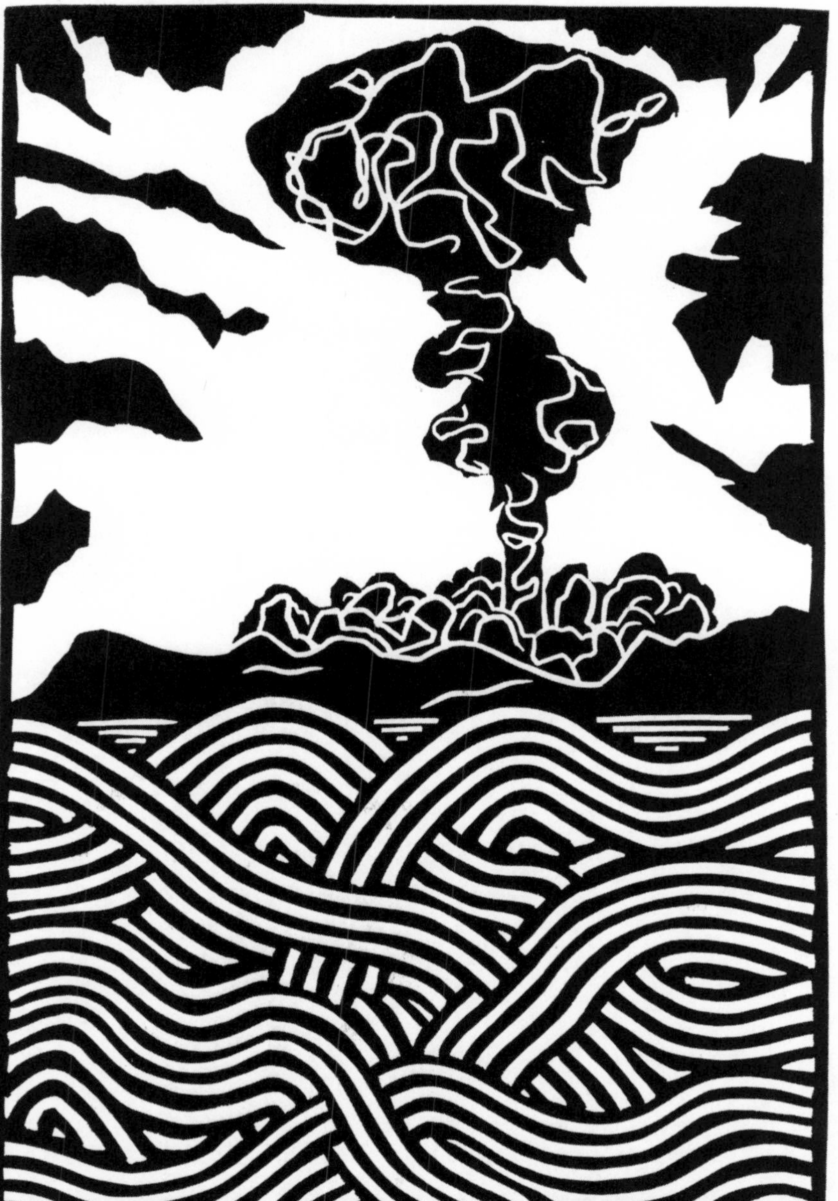

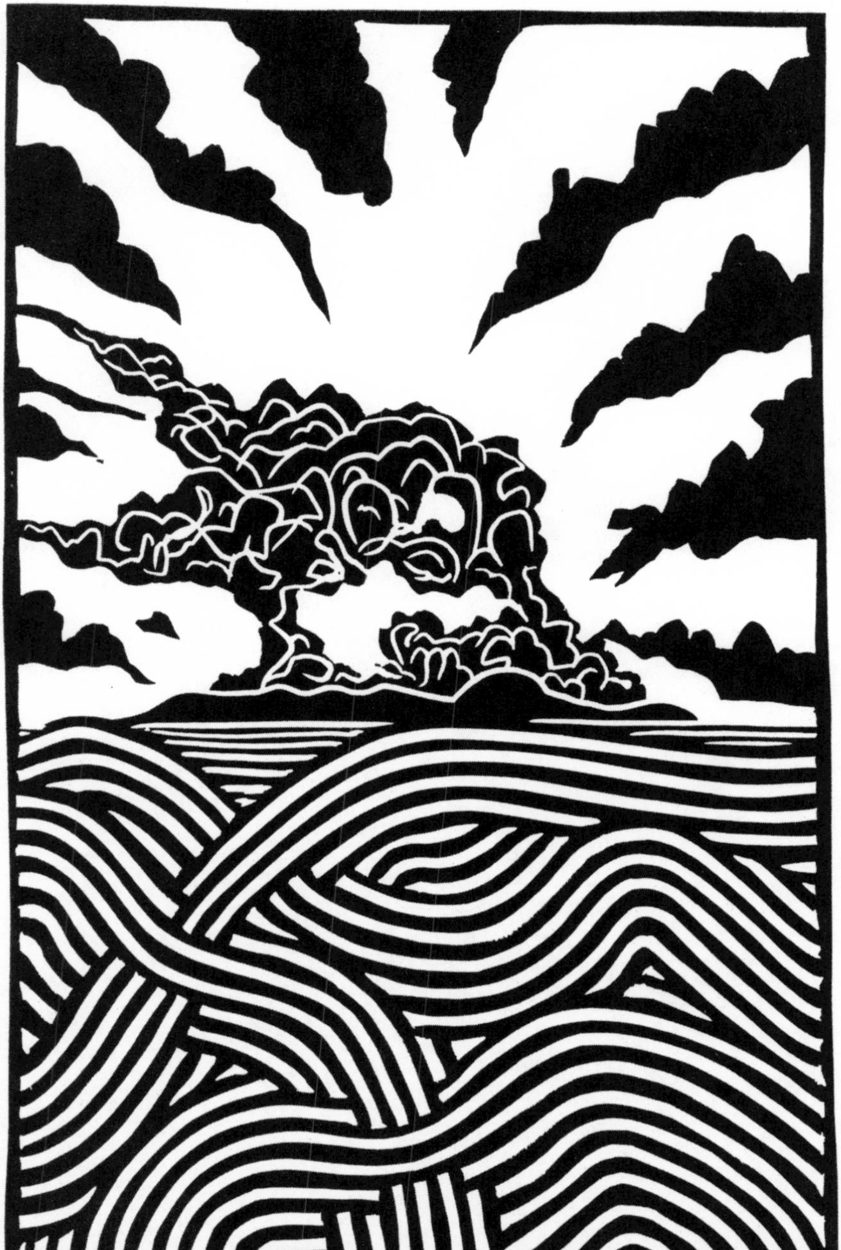

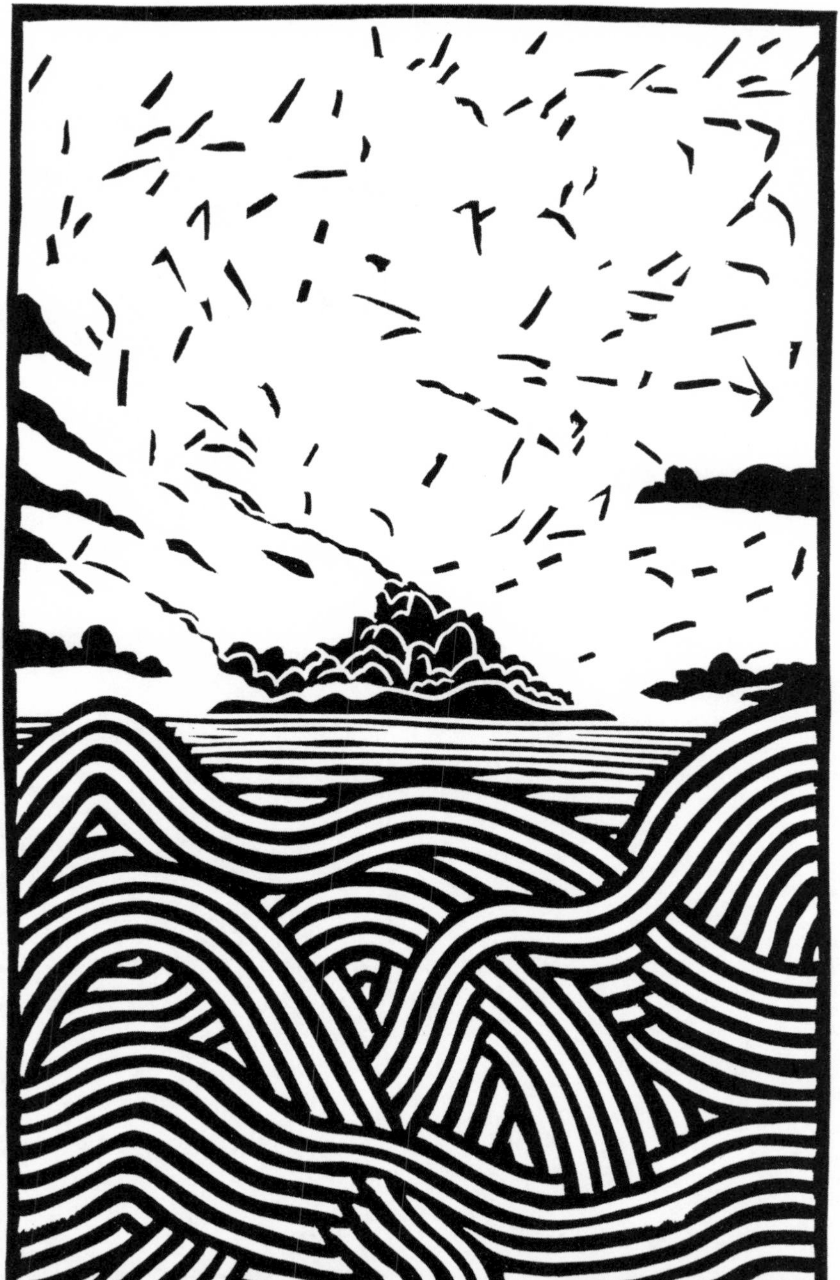

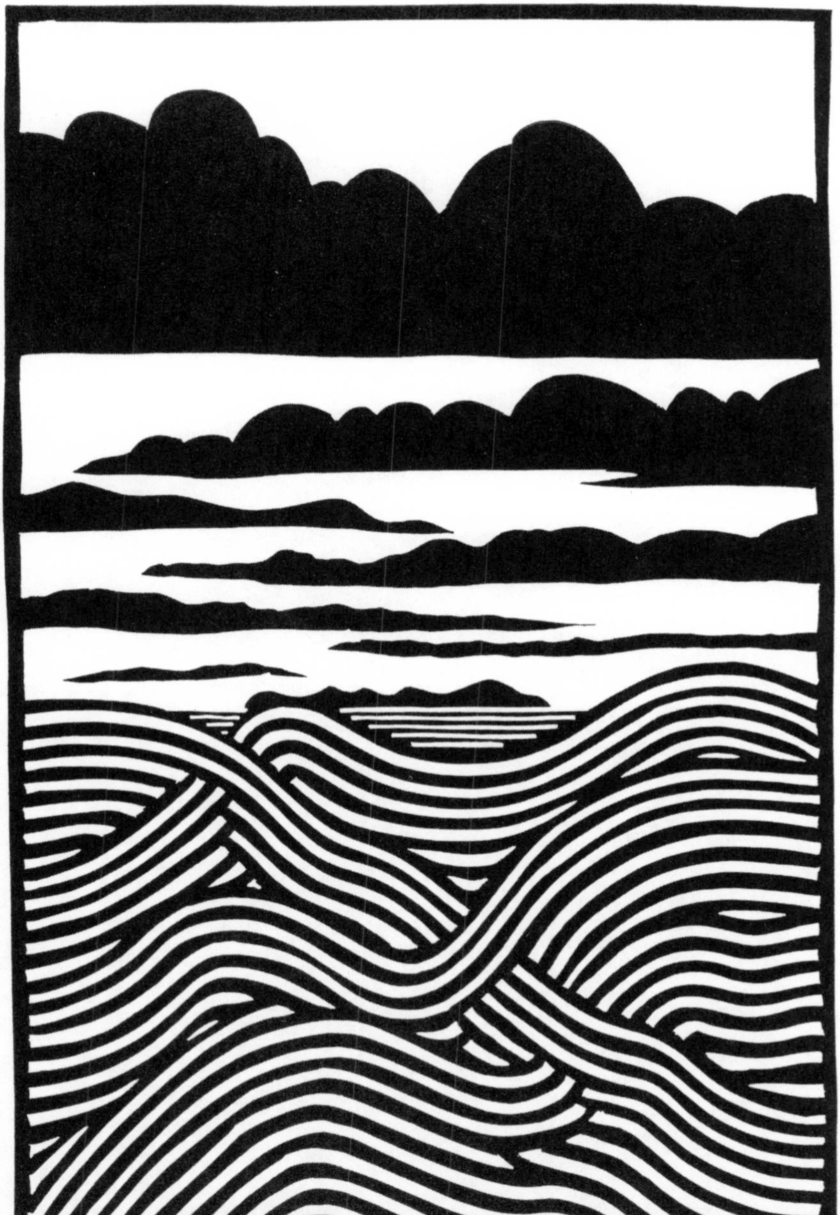

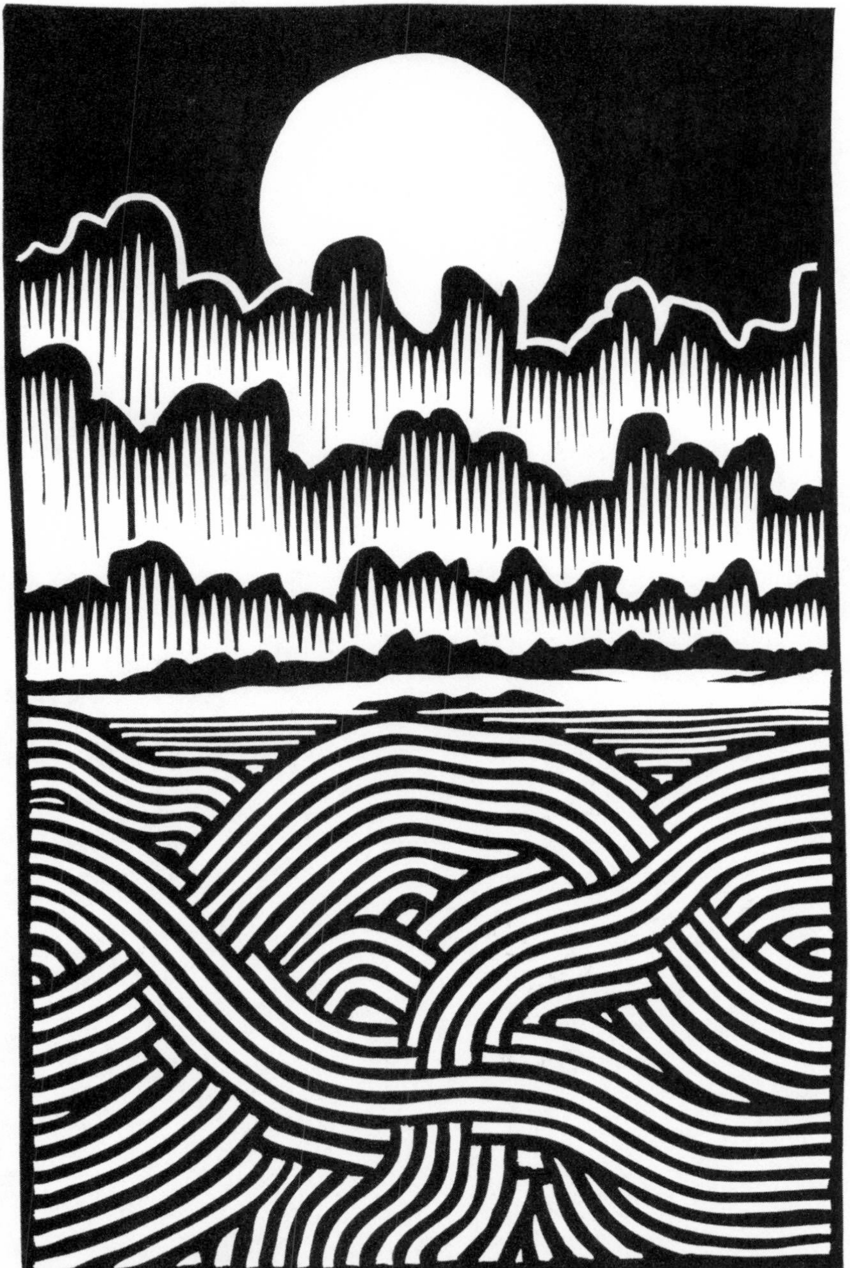

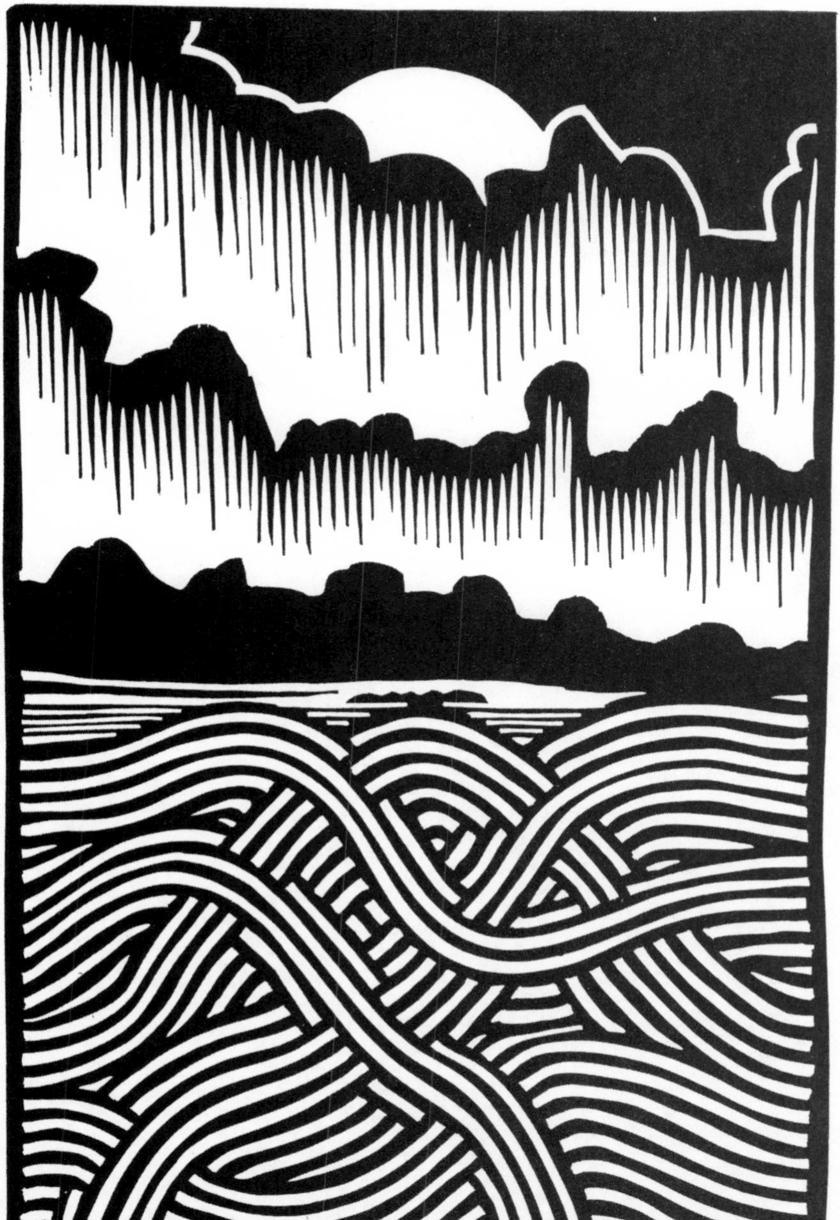

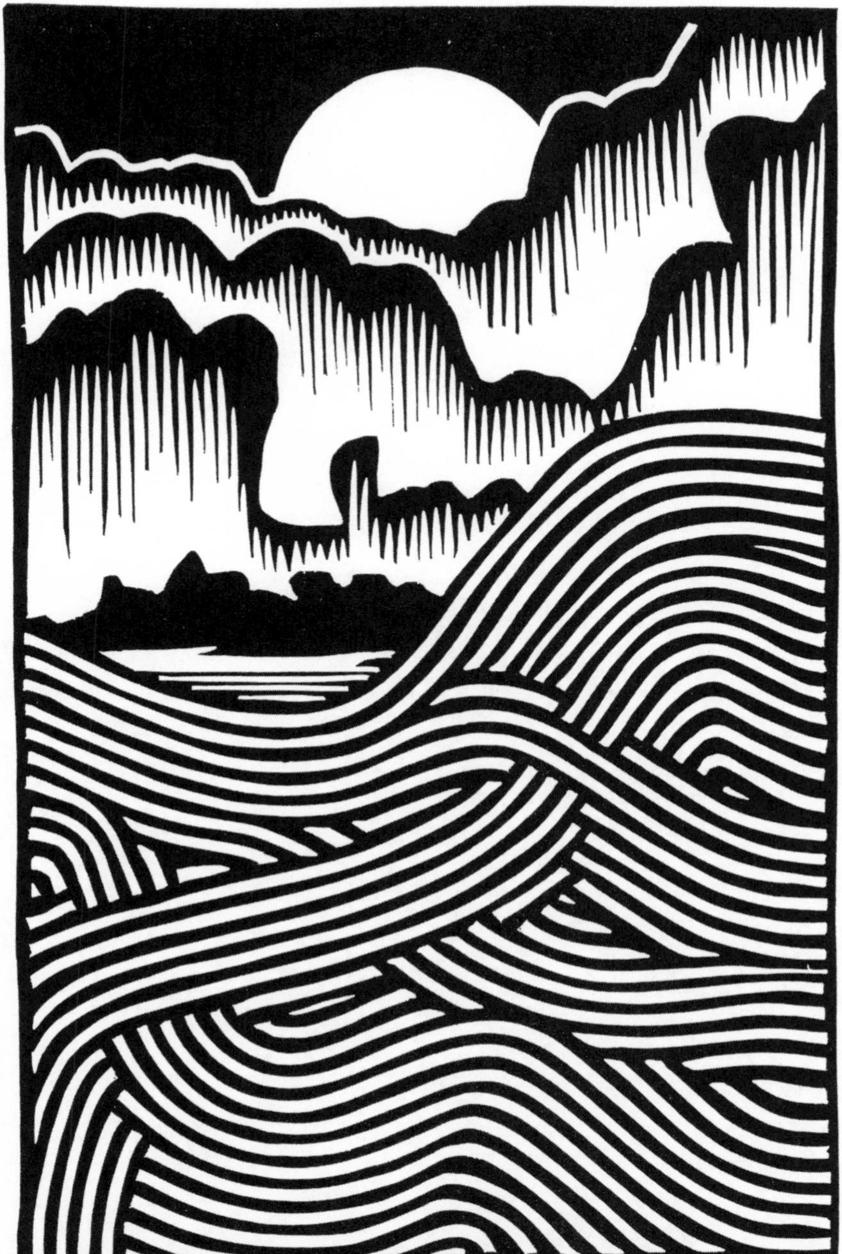

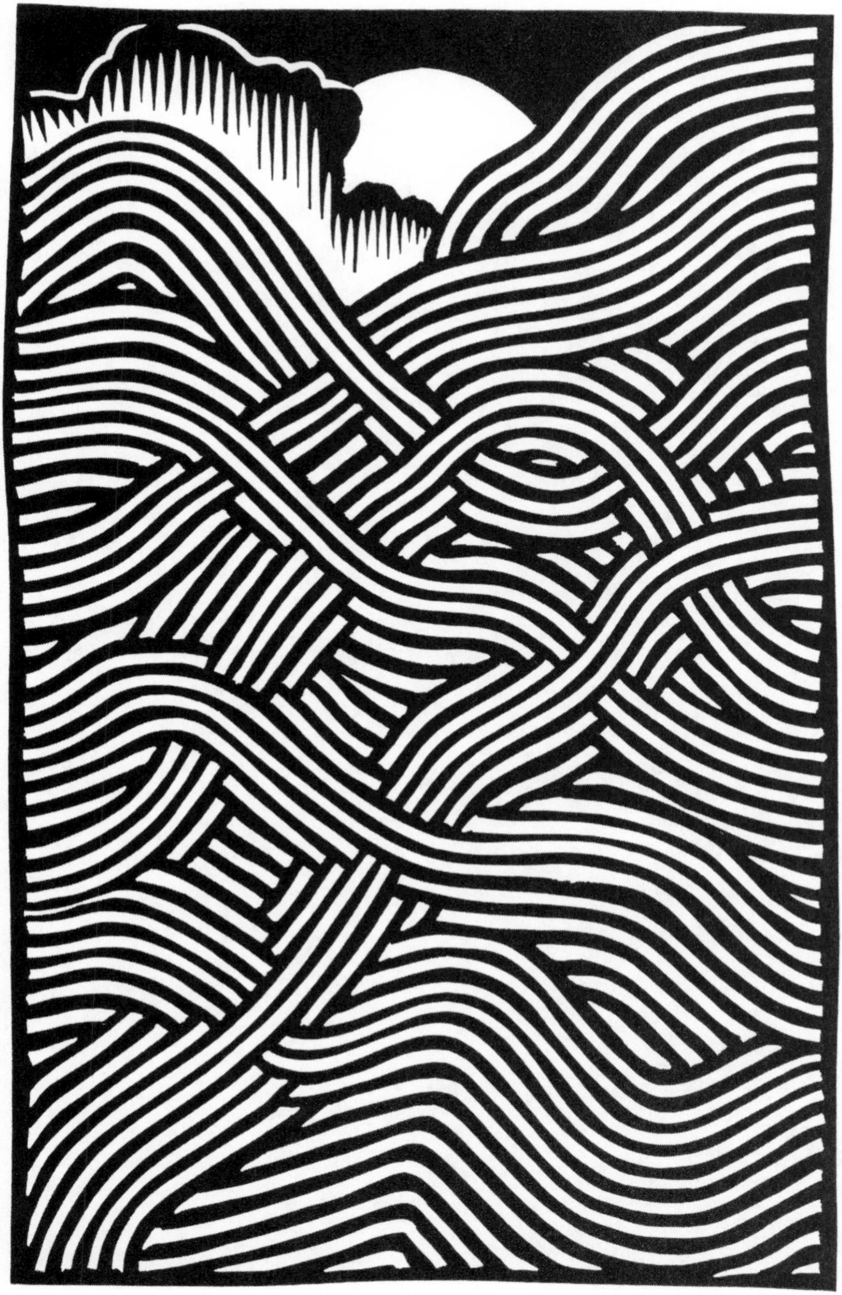

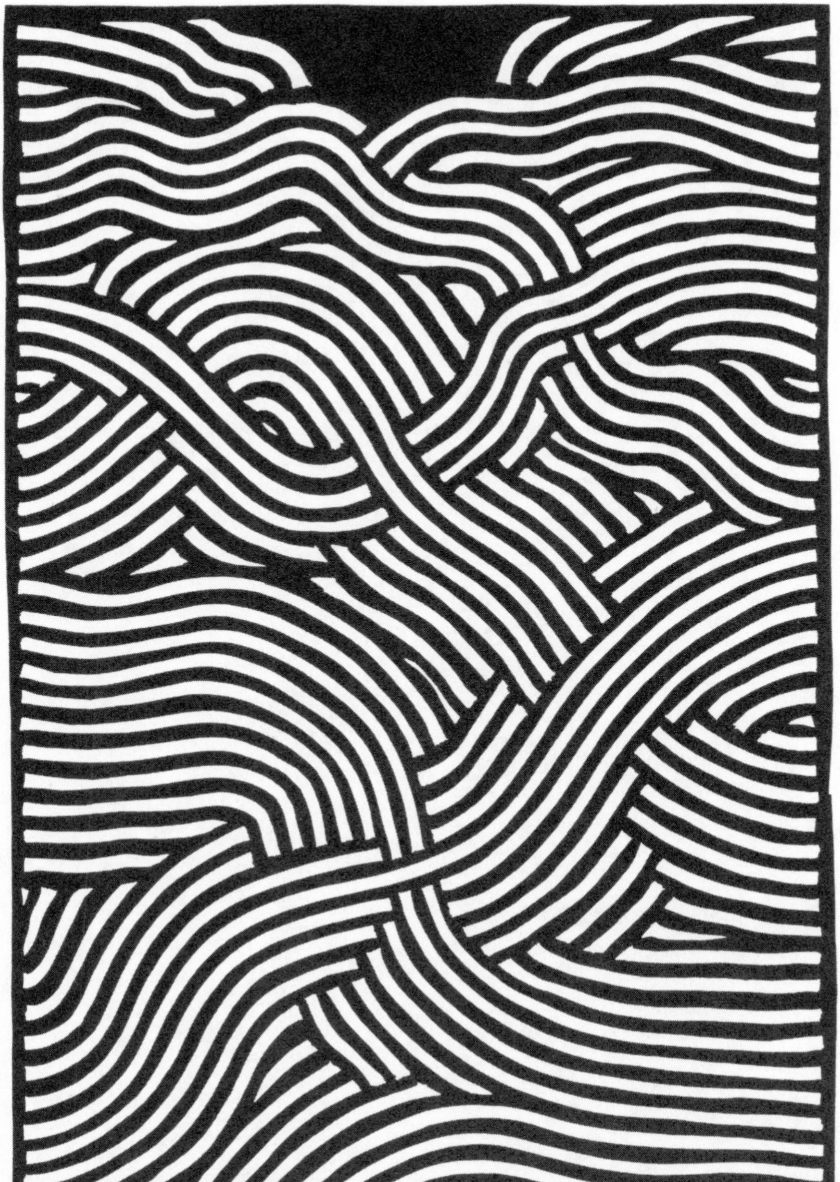

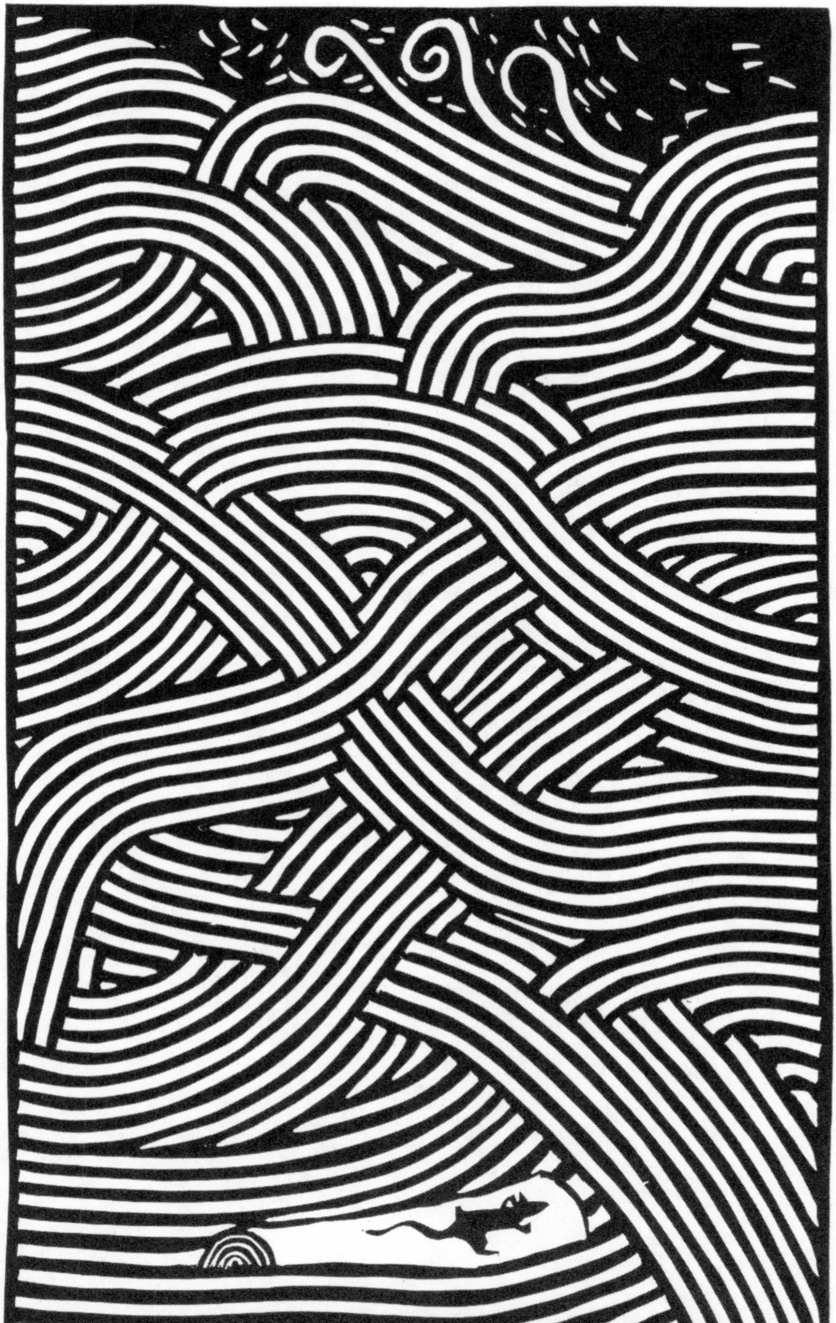

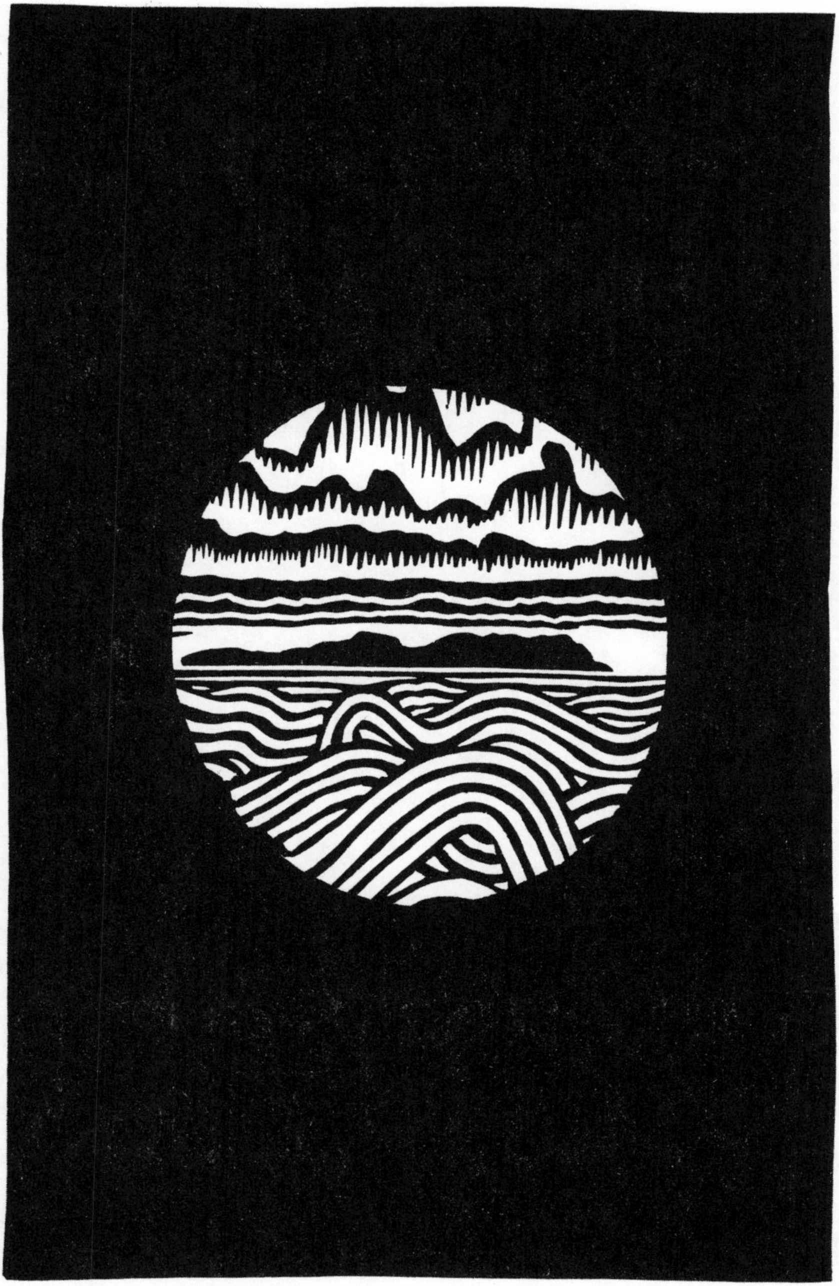

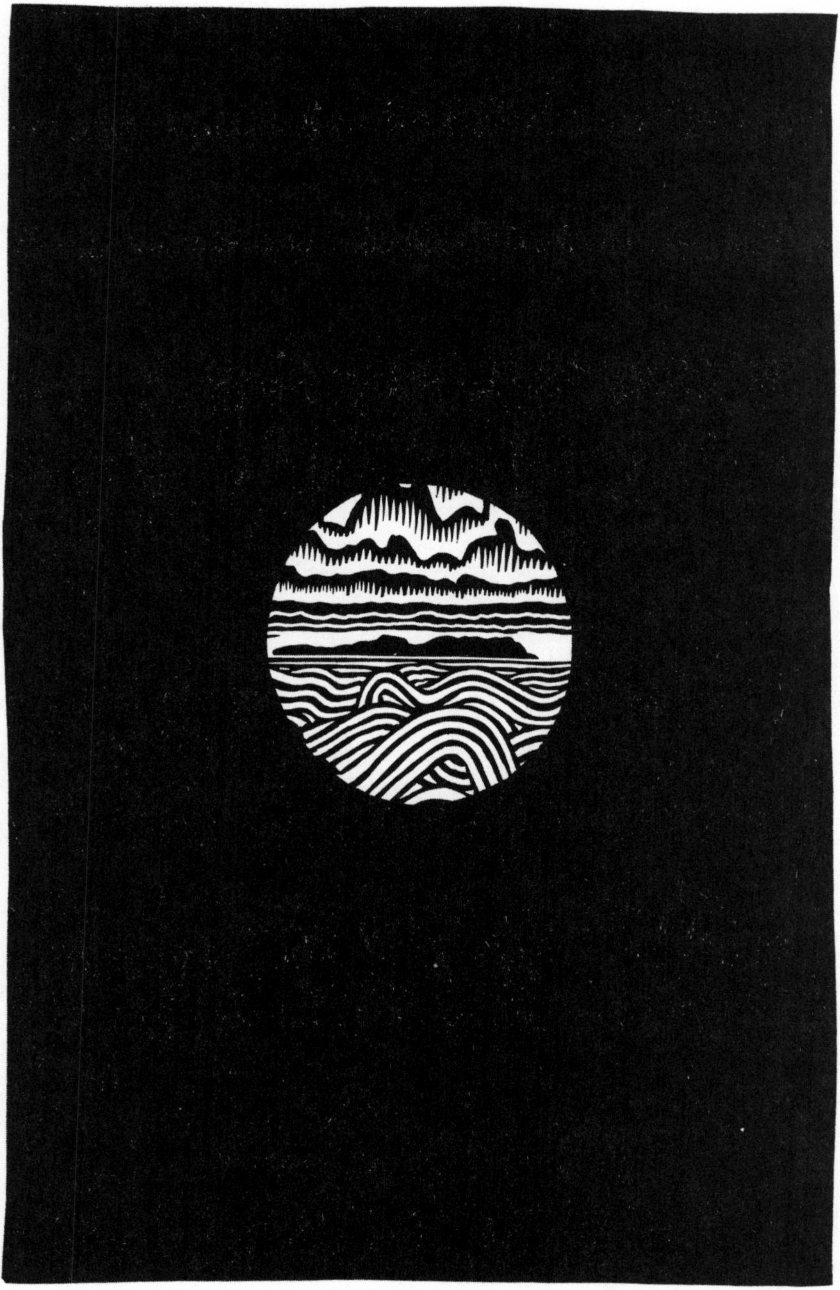

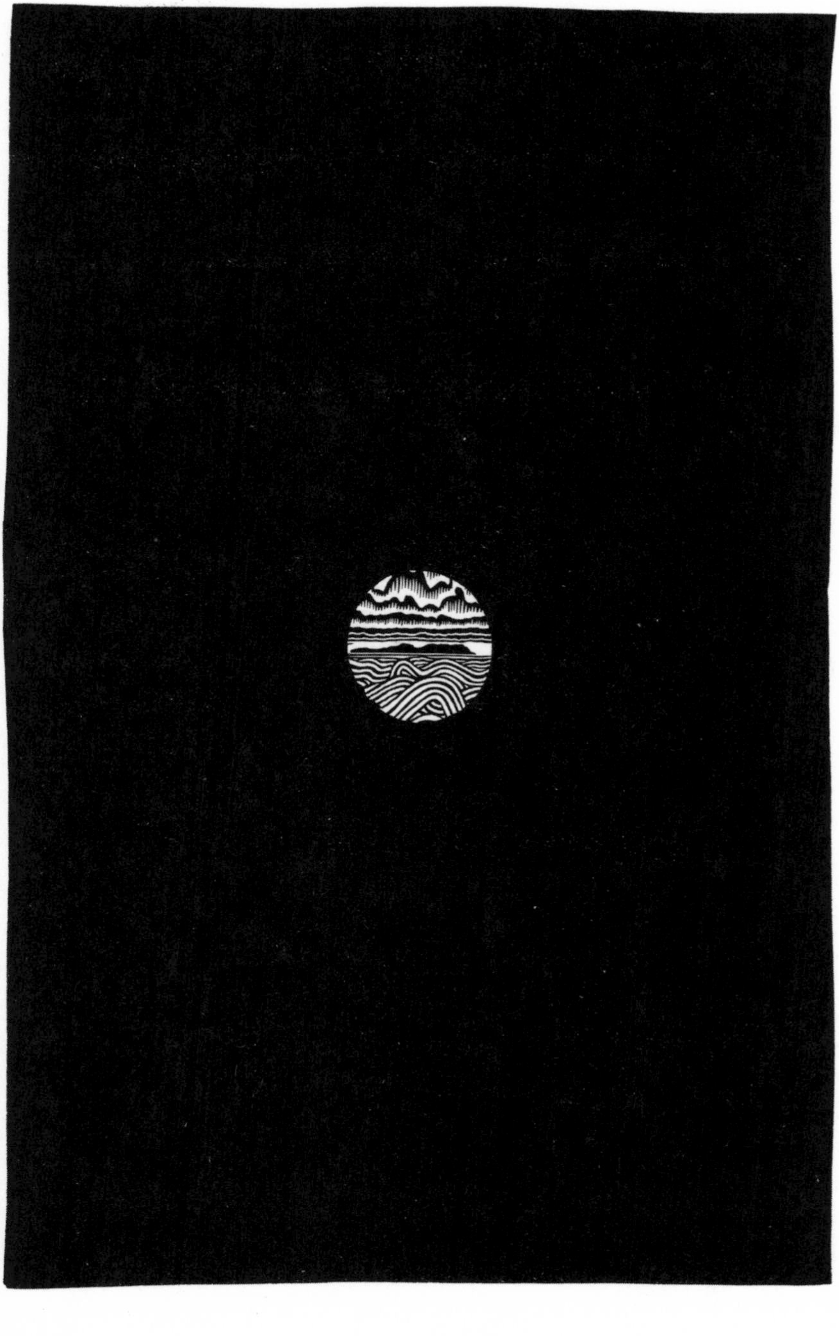